Summer 1956, a backyard gathering at 2840 Ridge Road. Copyright Meredith Corp.

This book is dedicated to Owl's Head residents - past, present, and future.

Owl's Head
A Hidden Gem

Sondra Ashmore, PhD

Christine Guzzo Vickery

Watercolors by
Sharon Larson

Contributions by
Julian and Jane Archer
Arnold Garson
Bill Ralston

Edited by
Kate Bruns

ISBN: 978-0-578-88757-9 (Hardcover)

Library of Congress Control Number: 2021906382

Front cover photo by Sondra Ashmore.

Printed by Sondra Ashmore Ink, in Des Moines, Iowa,
United States of America.

First printing edition 2021.

TABLE OF CONTENTS

Foreword

1 Nollen House

5 Tone Brothers Inc.

7 Witmer House

11 Langan Brothers Houses

15 Langan Paper Company

17 Rawson House

20 The Staff

21 Coffin House

25 Stevenson House

29 The Newspaper People Of Owl's Head

33 Gilcrest House

36 Gilcrest Lumber

37 Brecht House

41 Artists Of Owl's Head

47 Watt House

51 An Unlikely Neighbor

53 Atkins Weaver House

59 Sutherland House

63 A Musical Guest

67 Reynolds House

71 Harbach House

75 Corley House

79 Labor Day Party

85 Houses in Owl's Head

87 References

89 Acknowledgements

90 Authors and Illustrator

FOREWORD

By Sondra Ashmore

Although I grew up in Des Moines, it wasn't until my high school years that I found myself driving around with a friend south of Grand Avenue and discovered a magical neighborhood I had never encountered before. I was taken with the stunning historic homes hidden behind large apartment buildings, surrounded by trees and the prodigious former governor's mansion. At the time, I wasn't aware that the neighborhood had a name, Owl's Head, or of its standing as a National Historic District. I was, however, sure I had discovered a special place, but could never have predicted I'd be calling it my family's home twenty years later.

Compared to many historic districts, Owl's Head is small. It consists of 26 acres spanning four streets - 28th Street, Ridge Road, 29th Street, and Forest Drive. Most of the homes were designed by prominent architects of the late 19th and early 20th centuries: Liebbe, Nourse & Rasmussen, Proudfoot, Bird and Rawson (now Brooks Borg Skiles), Sawyer and Watrous, Kraetsch and Kraetsch, and C. C. Cross. While united by a

common era (1885 to1917), each home offers a unique style that reflects the lifestyles of the original owners and the adaptations subsequent homeowners have made to suit their preferences and the changing times.

It was the homes and quaintness of the neighborhood that initially captured my attention, but I have since come to understand that it is the stories of homeowners past that make Owl's Head a treasure. Many Des Moines pioneers chose to build homes in the new western streetcar suburb located south of Ingersoll Avenue near Greenwood park due to the ease of transportation to downtown and because cars were starting to increase in popularity. Bill Ralston shares the story of his great great uncles, W. H. and T. M. Langan, who were the founders of the Langan Paper Company and built homes next door to one another on 29th Street. John Tone shared his family's history of Tone Brothers, Inc. (now Tone's) and his many relatives who called Owl's Head home. The Gilcrests of Gilcrest Lumber Company (now

Gilcrest/Jewett) built three of the Owl's Head homes and were founding members of the Central Church of Christ in Des Moines, one of the oldest churches in the city. Owl's Head residents also played seminal roles in art, politics, and journalism. Arnold Garson, former resident and retired editor of the Des Moines Register, penned the fascinating story of how the people of Owl's Head helped shape the newspaper.

The most interesting and rewarding part of writing this book was the love and nostalgia that radiated from current and former residents as they told their stories of living in the neighborhood. They spoke of childhood friendships, holiday parties, weddings, adventures in third-floor ballrooms, home restorations, scandal, and mischief. One former resident, Ed Carpenter of 330 29th Street, stopped me by surprise while I was outside gardening and asked me about his childhood home. It didn't take me long to realize he was more than a casual admirer of historic homes, and he went on to share fun tales and photos from his time on 29th Street. A group of childhood friends stopped by to drop off photos for the book and laughed as they flipped through photos and spoke of the good times they had growing up in the neighborhood. I have the great privilege of living next door to the longest-term residents of Owl's Head, Julian and Jane Archer (52 years and counting), who spearheaded Owl's Head's National Historic District designation and have fought for preservation of the neighborhood. I feel honored that they contributed the story of their home and other valuable historical artifacts.

Researching the neighborhood has led me to the realization that some things have changed through the years while others have remained very much the same. Today you won't find many third floors used as ballrooms or horses in the carriage houses, nor will you find full-time staff living in the homes. You will, however, find families that have chosen to buy houses near one another and neighbors who still regularly socialize together. The long-standing Labor Day party is a strong testament to this

valued tradition. Professions represented over the years have included business owners, writers, architects, attorneys, doctors, insurance professionals, and even prominent politicians. The children still play together and sled down the hills behind 2908 Forest Drive. The once cutting-edge custom homes have aged like a fine wine into unique historic properties, and the pride of ownership has remained unwavering.

Capturing the history and beauty of Owl's Head has been an important mission for me. I would never have been able to make my vision a reality without bringing together the most amazing team possible. My aunt, Christine Vickery, who has published books on both genealogy and interior design, graciously agreed to sign on as a co-author. Sharon Larson, a supremely talented artist, captured the beauty in her stunning watercolor paintings. The sharp editorial eye of friend and former Owl's Head resident, Kate Bruns, made all the difference in refining the content and flow. Although I do wish I had the bandwidth to do in-depth research on every

home in the neighborhood, and would love to do so someday, I hope this book brings you some of the sense of wonder I felt on a drive through Owl's Head so many years ago.

Enjoy!

NOLLEN HOUSE | 402 29TH STREET

By Dr. Julian and Jane Archer

Owl's Head Historic District takes its name from a farm known as Owl's Head, which was located on the open flat land just west of what was then the edge of Des Moines in the second half of the 19th century.

The house at 402 29th Street sits on what was then and still is the widest lot in the Owl's Head Historic District. This unusually wide, 170-foot lot was needed because the developer, W. W. Witmer, moved his 1880 farmhouse, which sat where 2900 Grand Avenue is now, to the northwest corner of Lot 2, Langan Place (then known as Pierce's Subdivision; changed to Langan Place in 1924). At that time a frame house, whose style and existence are today something of a mystery, was located where 402 29th Street now sits. Though there may have been an appeal to having a wide lot, the presence of this very small, humble farmhouse and a frame house, which one can only assume was of modest quality, may have been the reason it took more than 30 years before anyone decided to build a more stately house there. Consequently, 402 29th Street was one of the last structures to be built in this lovely subdivision.

The lot was purchased by Gerard Nollen in 1914. As the 20th century unfolded in Des Moines, the Nollens emerged as one of the most prominent families in the city. Gerard graduated from Grinnell College in 1902 and followed his brother, Henry, into the insurance business. Both brothers were gifted mathematicians. Gerard went to work for Bankers Life in 1912, the same year Henry left the company to work for Equitable of Iowa. Two years later, Gerard married Helen Witmer, whose parents owned and developed the Owl's Head subdivision that had been incorporated into the city of Des Moines in 1890.

By the opening of the 20th century the appeal of large Victorian frame houses had passed, and W. W. and Mary Witmer, though wealthy, wanted to create something more unusual for the area. They built a stately Neo-Georgian Colonial structure on the corner of Grand Avenue and 29th Street in 1903, joining the other consequential residential mansions along Grand Avenue. When Gerard and Helen built a house of their own just south of her parents' house, they called upon one of Des Moines' premier

NOLLEN HOUSE (CONT.)

architectural firms, Sawyer and Watrous, to design a classical two-story Georgian Colonial house similar to, though smaller than, the one at 2900 Grand. Plans were drawn in 1915, bids solicited in 1916, and construction completed in 1917. But Gerard and Helen lived at 402 only a short while. W. W. Witmer had died in 1916, and when Mary died in 1921, Gerard and Helen sold their new residence to brother Henry and moved into 2900 Grand. The area was almost exclusively a Nollen enclave, as the two unmarried Nollen sisters also built a house in Owl's Head, at the southeast corner of 29th Street and Grand Avenue. There they resided and created a private school, as well as built an additional Nollen house just to the south.

The Nollen brothers played a critical role in establishing Des Moines as a great finance city. Gerard rose to head Bankers Life, today Principal Financial Group, and Henry became president of Equitable of Iowa, which became part of ING Insurance and today is Voya Financial. They took these companies from small local enterprises to major national players. With the revival of downtown Des Moines and the establishment of the Civic Center in 1979, the adjacent square was named Nollen Plaza in their honor. (When it was redeveloped in 2013, the name was changed to Cowles Commons.) A third Nollen brother, John S. Nollen, was on the faculty of Grinnell College and served as its president from 1931 to 1940.

Henry Nollen and his wife, Pearl, owned 402 longer than any other Nollen family members, occupying it until 1951 when it was sold to Iowa Secretary of State Melvin Synhorst, who treated it as an investment to flip. Synhorst split Lot 2 by severing the southern 120 feet, 402 and its garage, and selling it in 1952 to Deighton Smith, an architect. He sold the northern 50 feet, the farmhouse, to the Kalejs family in 1953. He also sold off the carved stone garden benches in the backyard sunken terrace and the leaded glass bookcases in the living room, items which had been part of the house since it was built.

Smith subsequently sold 402 in 1962 to Florence Cowles Kruidenier, who kept the house for two years and spent a considerable amount of money on restoration and repairs. The wealthy publishing heiress was known to have a passion for buying fine houses, restoring them, selling them, and then moving on to another restoration project. The home was next purchased by Robert Holt, the owner of Robin Hill Stables in the nearby Raccoon River Valley, who allowed it to fall into terrible disrepair, so much so that when it was sold to Richard O'Leary and his wife in July 1968 they decided not even to move in but to put it back on the market immediately.

That same month, Julian and Jane Archer came house-hunting in Des Moines because Julian had accepted a post at Drake University teaching European history. The Archers were determined to purchase, rather than rent, a residence. The first house they looked at was 450 29th Street,

and while they were viewing it they saw a "for sale" sign in the yard of the house next door at 402. They arranged to view it, and even after learning that the upstairs shower/bath leaked into the living room they made an offer. In August the Archers took title to the first residence they had ever owned.

The Archers now are the senior Owl's Head residents, having owned 402 for more than 50 years, and also the longest owners of any Owl's Head house in history. Their ownership has entailed renovating the entire house—ceilings, walls, floors, windows, roof, bathrooms, heating, electrical, and fencing. In 1990 they also purchased the northern 50 feet of Lot 2 Langan Place (446 29th Street) and have restored that house over the years.

When the Archers purchased 402 it was not evident, even among real estate agents, which way the Owl's Head area was headed socio-economically. Indeed, it seemed to be heading toward becoming an area of deterioration composed of houses divided up and converted into apartments, like the rundown Sherman Hill area and the 6th to 15th Street area north of University. The houses at 400 28th Street, 2838 Forest Drive, and 320 29th Street already had gone that way. Then in the mid-1970s the Nollen sisters' school, already completely converted into apartments, was purchased by a developer who wanted to build a twin tower apartment complex 13 and 11 stories high. This prompted the Owl's Head neighbors to coalesce in

opposition and take their objections to the Des Moines Planning Commission, which lopped off several stories of each building because the developer could not assure the commission that his original project would provide enough parking in or beside the twin buildings. The reduced height caused the developer to cancel his project. Realizing through the ordeal that Owl's Head had no real protection, the Archers organized with neighbors to seek National Register Historic District recognition for the area. The Archers spent a year soliciting an application and brief property history from each of the homeowners until, finally, all was in order. With the helpful endorsement of the State of Iowa Division of Historic Preservation in 1978, the application received city, state, and national approval, making Owl's Head Des Moines' first historic district. Shortly thereafter the City of Des Moines passed an ordinance authorizing the creation of a Historic District Commission with the power to compel residents to follow historic restoration guidelines, and

then Owl's Head residents requested that their district participate in and fall under the direction of this commission.

The establishment of the Historic District was the turning point for the prestige of Owl's Head. Property values dramatically increased, owners began spending significant sums to improve their properties, and the already-divided residences returned to single-family dwellings.

A scarcely-noticed expansion to the neighborhood occurred in 1994. This was the addition of a 46-foot-wide strip of undeveloped land to the west of 2908 Forest and 304, 320, 330, 338, and 402 29th Street. This area had been the site of a World War II Victory Garden, which had continued to function as a community garden into the 1980s. The land was tilled each spring and parceled out at no charge to those who wanted to plant there. It was an open, fertile terrain from which neighbors harvested abundant organic produce well before

what became known as organic cultivation came into vogue. The expansion came about because the former garden area was a landlocked parcel behind 2910 Grand Avenue that was put up for bids by its owner, the Catholic Chancery. The bordering Owl's Head landowners, several of whom were attorneys, agreed among themselves to bid $1,000 over whatever the highest bid was and made that their offer. The only other bidders were Matt and Kay Bucksbaum, who owned a large lot to which their house stood adjacent. The Bucksbaums' attorney immediately contested the Owl's Head bid, claiming an improper bidding process. This resulted in a legal stalemate spreading over three years with exchanges of letters and arguments among the attorneys. Since the Archers knew the Bucksbaums personally, they invited them over to discuss the impasse and arrived at an agreeable price, bypassing all the arguments raised by the attorneys and the 29th Street lots were expanded.

Tone Brothers, Inc.

Those little red spice jars that line your shelves have strong connections to Owl's Head, home to the family that founded what is today North America's oldest spice company.

Three Tone siblings, Jehiel, Isaac (I. E.), and Marcia, moved to Des Moines in the early 1870s to start a new life in Iowa. Marcia settled in Des Moines with her new husband, Thomas M. Langan, who went on to found the Langan Paper Company. Brothers Jehiel and I. E. moved to Des Moines in 1873 to start a spice company, Tone Brothers, Inc., in a building on Court Avenue that spanned two storefronts. The original Tone Brothers building was on the land where the Civic Center currently resides.

The rise in popularity of Tone Brothers, Inc. spices was premised on their commitment to quality and innovation. While many spice producers at the time included ground walnuts or olive stones in their black pepper for texture, Tone Brothers was the first to use 100% ground pepper in the United States. Their early business also included coffee, and they were the first to produce and sell roasted coffee west of the Mississippi River. The Tone family traveled extensively around the world to procure the best ingredients possible for their products.

Jay Tone Sr., son of I. E. Tone, joined the company in 1897 after graduating with a degree in chemical engineering from the Massachusetts Institute of Technology. Armed with a passion

for ingenuity and the drive to take his family's company forward into the next century, he ultimately was awarded 40 patents and contributed the idea of offering extracts, inspired by a college friend who worked in the extract business. His most notable invention was the circulation extract percolator used in both the food extraction and pharmaceutical industries. Despite his immense impact on the company, he was not promoted to the role of president until 1939. He led the company for 40 years, until the age of 96, giving him a 73-year tenure. Tone Brothers, Inc. was sold to Mid-Continent Bottlers in 1968, then was spun off to Universal Foods in 1976. It has since changed ownership several times and is currently headquartered in

Ankeny, Iowa. Tone's, as it is now simply known, celebrated its 100-year anniversary in 1973 with commemorative tins that replicated the original tins from 1873.

The Tone family was fond of Owl's Head and has resided in four different homes in the neighborhood. Jay Tone, who was born the year his father and uncle started Tone Brothers, Inc., was the first Tone family member to live in Owl's Head. He married W. W. Witmer's daughter, Mabel Witmer, in 1903 in the Witmer home at 2900 Grand Avenue. They moved into the Witmer's farm house at 450 29th Street, directly south of the home at 2900 Grand, after their wedding. There they started raising their

children, Jay Jr. and Mary. They later moved into 2900 Grand and lived there until 1924, when they moved nearby to 35th Street.

Jay's uncle, Thomas Langan, and cousin, Grace Tone Langan, built the house at 338 29th Street in 1907. His aunt, Marcia (Tone) Langan had passed away before having a chance to live in the neighborhood.

The last Tone family members to move into Owl's Head, Jay's parents I. E. and Betsy Tone, built a custom brick home and carriage house designed by Frederick Wallich at 2849 Forest Drive at the northeast corner of Forest Drive and 29th Street.

WITMER HOUSE | 2900 GRAND AVENUE

There's one address exception to the rule defining Owl's Head as 28th Street, 29th Street, Ridge Road, and Forest Drive: The stately Witmer House at 2900 Grand Avenue. Perhaps the most widely recognized Owl's Head residence, the 1903 Neo-Georgian Colonial home on the corner of 29th Street and Grand Avenue was designed by Liebbe, Norse, & Rasmussen. The lot was originally home to a farmhouse that at the turn of the century was moved just south of the new home at 2900 Grand. That farmhouse still stands today at 450 29th Street and is credited as the oldest home in the neighborhood.

2900 Grand contributed to the impressive collection of architectural masterpieces that lined Grand Avenue west of downtown and is one of a handful that remains today. The home was built by William Wirt (W. W.) and Mary Witmer. The Witmers purchased the property in 1880 along with much of the land west of Terrace Hill and south of Grand Avenue. They owned most, but not all, of the land that today makes up Owl's Head Historic District.

W. W. Witmer's career started in law and quickly expanded to newspapers. [See the Newspaper People of Owl's Head chapter for additional details]. He invested in land west of downtown and developed not only Owl's Head, but other areas north of Grand Avenue. He co-founded the New England Loan and Trust Company focusing on farm mortgages. He was also part of the team that built the Savery II Hotel and eventually became the controlling owner. Witmer was also a partner in the Eureka Coal and Mining Company.

WITMER HOUSE (CONT.)

The sprawling brick home features a circular portico with rounded leaded glass windows. The scallop shell motif above the center second floor balcony is reminiscent of another Liebbe, Norse, & Rasmussen design in Owl's Head at 331 28th Street. A Palladian stained glass window at the top of the stairway adds dramatic color to the entry of the home. A large white fireplace takes center stage in the living room, a nod to the status of the Witmer family. The home includes a spacious covered porch for outdoor entertaining on the east side. It has since been enclosed for an additional indoor space. An expansive dining room to the front of the home allowed ample space for family meals and parties. Upstairs the sitting room overlooks the portico and the front lawn. There is a porte-cochère on the south side of the home for carriage arrivals.

The Witmers continued to live in the home, and both of their daughters were married there. Their oldest daughter, Mabel, married Jay Tone of Tone Brothers, Inc. [See the Tone Brothers, Inc. chapter for additional details], and younger daughter, Helen, married Gerard Nollen, president of Bankers Life and the namesake of the former Nollen Plaza in downtown Des Moines. Helen and Gerard Nollen's daughters, Johanna and Sara (Sally), were also married in the home. W. W. died in the home in 1916, and Mary passed away five years later. Upon their parents' deaths, the Tones moved into 2900 Grand and the Nollens built a house just south of the farmhouse at 402 29th Street. Gerard and Helen moved into the home after the Tones left in 1924 and lived there until 1947. Helen died there in 1940, and after several years Gerard decided it was too much house for one person.

Nollen's sale of the family home started a new era for 2900 Grand as the state was searching for a permanent home for its governor. The residence was ultimately purchased as the new governor's mansion in December 1947 at a price of $27,200. The State of Iowa hired architect J.W. Brooks, Fane F. Vawter Construction Company, and designers from Killians of Cedar Rapids to spend a year updating and furnishing the home at a cost of just over $22,000. Iowa's 31st governor, William Beardsley, and first lady, Charlotte Beardsley, moved into the home at the start of his term in January 1949. The 1953 February/March issue of The Iowan noted four rooms on the main floor (library, living room, dining room, and kitchen), five bedrooms on the second floor in addition to a sitting room, and two bedrooms on the third floor for staff. The home had three full-time staff - a maid,

Far Right: View of the Palladian style window at the landing in the main stairway, 2020

Right: The formal living room, 2020

housekeeper/cook, and a yardsman. The home came furnished with everything the first family needed from bedding to kitchen utensils, and, according to the first lady, "moving in was as easy as bringing in your suitcases." It ultimately was home to the families of five additional governors including Leo Hoegh, Herschel Loveless, Norman Erbe, Harold Hughes, and Robert Ray. Eric Miller, formerly of 2900 Forest Drive, recalled "Both the Ray family and the Hughes family were down-to-earth, thoughtful and real people. I have fond memories of Harold Hughes personally answering the door and providing the treats at Halloween, and of Bob Ray and his family biking through the neighborhood and socializing regularly. He had a state trooper who drove him to the Capitol Building each morning, and he was humble enough to sit up front to avoid the 'limo look.' The Ray girls had a trampoline and would gladly invite their neighbors to join in."

In 1971, the Hubbell family donated their family's stately home six blocks east of 2900 Grand at 2300 Grand (also known as Terrace Hill) to the State of Iowa. It was decided it would serve as both a museum and the official home of the governor. Governor Ray and his family moved from 2900 Grand to the third floor of Terrace Hill in 1976, raising concern by the Owl's Head Neighborhood Association about the fate of the home. Many of the large historic homes on Grand Avenue were being torn down to build apartments or commercial buildings. Owl's Head residents went to state officials, including the governor, pleading to have the character of the home at 2900 Grand preserved and asking that it not be converted to apartments. The state officials agreed, and a stipulation was made that the home could be converted to commercial use, but had to retain its exterior appearance. The home was sold to the Iowa Girls' High School Athletic Union in 1977 for the price of $150,000. The Iowa High School Speech Association was also headquartered there.

The Iowa Girls' High School Athletic Union eventually sold the home in late 2012 to John Beard, an experienced historic preservationist who has returned it to a single-family home. Beard and his husband, Mark Harrington, were married in the home in the tradition of many of Witmer and Nollen homeowners before them. The expansive dining room table and chairs used by the governors has been retained, and a large painting of the home gives a nod to the past as you walk in the front door.

Above Left: W. H. Langan house at 330 29th Street

Above Right: T. M. Langan House at 338 29th Street

Far Left: Frances Langan, wife of W. H. Langan, in her parlor at 330 29th St., 1908. Courtesy of Lewis & Clark College Aubrey Watzek Library Special Collections & Archives

Left: Ed Carpenter and Tim Rawson outside of 330 29th Street, December 31, 1954

LANGAN BROTHER HOUSES | 330 AND 338 29TH STREET

The family atmosphere of today's Owl's Head neighborhood is the product of strong tradition -- a tradition that included the brothers William Harrison (W. H.) and Thomas Mason (T. M.) Langan. The Langan brothers always preferred living near one another and remained close throughout their lives. They first built homes together on West Ninth Street in Des Moines: W. H. at 1160 and T. M. at 1193. During their stay in these homes, T. M. worked with C. H. Del Worth and J. H. Long to establish Nash Park on University Avenue between Ninth and Tenth Streets. He also started what would become Langan Brothers Paper Company with J. F. Rollins. W. H. later joined them as president and treasurer, with T. M. remaining as vice president.

W. H. and his wife, Frances Toan Langan, had four children: Mabel, John, Charles, and Lewis, all of whom pre-deceased their parents at a young age. Marcia Tone Langan was T. M.'s first wife and mother to his only child, Grace. Marcia's brothers Jehiel and I. E. Tone started Tone Brothers, Inc., [See the Tone Brothers, Inc. chapter for additional information], a Des Moines spice company still operating today. Marcia died at the young age of 57, and her funeral was held at their Ninth Street home. Living near one another offered the Langan brothers comfort during the untimely deaths of their family members. Neither of the early Langan homes on Ninth Street is still standing today.

Later in life, the brothers purchased adjacent properties in a popular new streetcar suburb on the west side of Des Moines: Owl's Head. W. H. and his family purchased the 330 lot on 29th Street; T. M. and his second wife, Julia, purchased the 338 lot. They shared a carriage house across both of their lots in which they stored W. H.'s carriage and T. M.'s car. While the homes are close in proximity and both built in 1907, the styles of their two houses could not be more different. W. H.'s house was brick and designed in the Tudor style, while T. M.'s was Medieval Rectilinear in style. Both homes boast large front porch sitting areas and prominent fireplaces in their formal living rooms.

Far Left: W. H. Langan (in top hat) stands between the Tone brothers (back row); T. M. Langan stands next to his wife, Julia (front row), 1910. Courtesy of Lewis & Clark College Aubrey Watzek Library Special Collections & Archives

Left: Sisters Cynthia and Connie Carpenter with a high school friend on the front porch at 330 29th Street, 1952

Left: T. M. and Julia Langan in their library at 338 29th St., 1916 Courtesy of Lewis & Clark College Aubrey Watzek Library Special Collections & Archives

Above: Drake Relays co-founder Robert Evans and wife Marjorie Evans admire a Drake Relays program, 1948

LANGAN BROTHER HOUSES (CONT.)

Given their connection to the paper and wood industries, the homes are appointed with quality woodwork. Matching butler pantries were included in both homes, although only the pantry in W. H.'s house remains. Their vestibules have similar tile patterns, but little else in the homes suggests they were designed to look alike.

W. H. died in September 1920 and T. M. died 10 months later. Their deaths both made front-page news in the Des Moines Register due to their prominence in the community. Their funerals were held in their Owl's Head homes. W. H.'s funeral was officiated by the president of Grinnell College due to his endowment for the Langan Hall dormitory and generosity to the college. Famed actor, Gary Cooper, lived in Langan Hall when he attended Grinnell College during the 1920s.

Far Right: Front entry at T. M. Langan home, 2017

Right: Living room and study at T. M. Langan home, 2017

Edwin and Wilma Carpenter and their children, Cynthia, Connie, and Edwin moved into 330 29th in 1944 and resided there until 1973. Edwin Carpenter was an attorney with Bannister, Carpenter, Ahlers & Cooney and was the only approved municipal bond attorney in Iowa for many years. He was the first of many attorneys to call 330 29th home. His grandfather, William L. Carpenter, was an early Des Moines pioneer and served as mayor from 1888 to 1890. Given Des Moines' relatively small size during that time, he was likely an associate of the original owner of the home, W. H. Langan. The residence at 330 29th has continued to be a home to attorneys including Tom McCollum and more recently Rob Sand who has pivoted into politics and is currently serving as the State Auditor. Sand's sister, Jen, also lived in Owl's Head at 407 28th Street keeping with the neighborhood tradition of family members living nearby.

Five years after T. M.'s death, his home was sold to Bob and Minnow Evans. Bob was a celebrated football player from Drake University who was also one of the founders of the Drake Relays and the event's first clerk. The Evanses hosted large parties in their home during the Drake Relays festivities each year. Their daughter, Ruth, lived in two other Owl's Head homes during her lifetime: 446 29th Street and 2832 Ridge Road. Bob Evans was a partner at the insurance firm Witmer-Kauffman-Evans in Des Moines. Bob and Minnow would be happy to know that the current owner of 338 29th Street was a record-setting Drake Relays champion who named her eldest son, Drake, after the event. Her youngest son, Dane, was born during the Drake Relays.

The Evans family remained at 338 29th for four decades, and the Crane family purchased the home in the early 1960s. Fred Crane was a professor at Drake University, and Anne taught sewing on Mary Jane Chinn's television show on KRNT Channel 8 from 1956 to 1968. The show catered to "modern Central Iowa homemakers." Fred and Anne raised their family in the home, lovingly maintained lavish landscaping, and worked tirelessly to keep the home in top condition.

In 2017, 338 29th was part of the Salisbury House Foundation's Holly and Ivy holiday tour along with the home at 2800 Ridge Road. During the tour, a photo of T. M. and Julia Langan sitting in the home's library was featured along with the home's history. The T. M. Langan home has been featured in Welcome Home Des Moines and HGTV magazines.

LANGAN BROTHERS CO.

118, 120. 122 THIRD STREET

DES MOINES,   IOWA.

Founded in 1876, the Langan Brothers Company—or Langan Paper Company, as it was later known—developed into one of Des Moines' largest businesses and also the largest and longest-standing paper company in Iowa. T. M. Langan left Chapin, Merritt, & Co. in 1876 to start the business with J. F. Rollins. In 1886, W. H. purchased J. F. Rollins' interest in the company and became president, with T. M. becoming vice president. It was at this time that the name changed to Langan Brothers Company.

They started as a small-scale paper business, specializing in the sale of blank books, paper bags, twine, and stationery. The business, begun on a small scale, was developed substantially along well-defined lines of labor and in accordance with the strictest commercial ethics. Promptness and reliability were always characteristic of the house in its dealings with its patrons.

LANGAN PAPER COMPANY

By Bill Ralsten

By 1900 the firm had become one of the largest wholesale paper companies in the Midwest. The Langans' business principles included cooperation and advancing loyal employees. That year it changed its business structure, incorporating an equity value of $75,000, and three long-time employees besides W. H. and T. M. Langan became shareholders. In addition to W. H. and T. M., the directors became George Voorhees, Fred Townsend, and Charles Pierce.

Soon after the restructuring, the company's office at 209-211 Walnut Street suffered a catastrophic loss from a fire caused by an electrical wiring problem. The fire destroyed its inventory -- which for a wholesale business is everything. The loss was fully insured and the company survived, but it must have been touch and go to keep customers from moving permanently to other suppliers. The fire also forced a community-wide discussion on needed changes to Des Moines commercial building codes.

In 1905, the brothers moved the 24-year-old business to a large brick warehouse at 188-120-122 Third Street. The building, built in 1892 for a farm implement and wagon dealer, stood for 96 years until a windstorm in 1988 caused the building to partially collapse, leading to its demolition.

The business continued to grow, and in 1908 the firm filed an amendment to its articles of incorporation, increasing its equity to $150,000.

After W. H. and T. M. both died in the 1920s, executives that had joined the firm in the 1880s continued to lead the company. Several worked there for more than 50 years--including Frank Townsend, who was ultimately associated with the firm for 66 years after joining in 1888 as a Teamster and rising through the ranks to become president and later chairman of the board.

At some point in its history—perhaps after the two Langan brothers died—Langan Paper became an employee-owned firm with all shares owned by employees participating in the company's profit-sharing and pension plans. By the 1940s the company had grown to 60 full-time employees and 7,000 dealers.

Langan Paper continued to operate until the late 1960s, 40 years after the brothers had passed away. The wholesale paper business is a very competitive, low-margin business where success depends on offering a strong range of paper and paper-related products and building a dominant market position in key cities and towns. Later in the 20th century the company stopped growing, and without size or a special advantage it couldn't survive. Langan Paper ultimately got bigger, but it did so by selling out to another firm. In 1974, the John Leslie Paper Company of Minnesota purchased Langan Paper after 98 years of business. The Leslie Paper Company was then acquired by International Paper Company in June of 1991.

RAWSON HOUSE | 2908 FOREST DRIVE

At the corner of 29th Street and Forest Drive in Owl's Head sits the home of renowned architect and Des Moines pioneer Harry Dustan Rawson. Rawson started designing his gabled cottage-style home at 2908 Forest Drive in 1890, but it was not built until 1904. He designed at least five additional homes in Owl's Head, including one prairie-style home at 431 28th Street, while with the architectural firm Proudfoot, Bird, and Rawson (now BBS Architects | Engineers). He designed a home on Forest Drive east toward Terrace Hill that is a near-replica of the home he built for his family at 2908 Forest Drive. It is unclear why he would have wanted a house nearly identical to his a mere two blocks away. Other notable buildings he designed in Des Moines include the Equitable Building, Rawson and Co. Apartment Building, Hotel Fort Des Moines, Masonic Temple of Des Moines, and Carnegie Library at

Drake University. He also designed many of the schools in Des Moines, including Roosevelt and Lincoln high schools, Callanan, Wilson, Irving, and Hiatt middle schools, as well as Greenwood elementary school. Greenwood, Callanan, and Roosevelt are today the public schools that serve the Owl's Head children. All of these buildings were designed while Rawson was residing on Forest Drive. Rawson's partner, J. Woolson Brooks, described Rawson as ". . . born into an 'old' family which exercised unidentified controls regarding civic development. He represented the epitome of the upper class, which now bugs the populist, consumerist, socialist segment of society. He was not a genius, nor a commanding personality, but he was affluent, socially elite, and possessed of mannerisms which produced the result he desired in others. He would have been considered influential in his day. His objectives were to maintain the status quo of his time."

Rawson's daughter, Mary Scott Rawson, married Richard Rollins at the home on June 26, 1928. At the bottom of the hill behind the porch was a large enclosed garden former resident Bill Eddy described "There were small [concrete] steps down from the back porch door of the house to the opening in the hedge." It is possible that the wedding took place in the garden or on the expansive back porch. Rollins was a member of the prominent Rollins family who built the Rollins mansion on the south side of downtown Des Moines. They were close associates with Carl Weeks, who built the Salisbury House and shared a love for traditional English architecture and landscaping. This was not the last wedding held at the home. The Eddy Family, second owners who resided there for more than 40 years, held their daughter's wedding in the home in 1989.

Far Left: Theodore Roosevelt High School architectural rendering, building design by Proudfoot, Bird and Rawson, 1924

Left: Eddy family enjoying a snowy day at 2908 Forest Drive, where sledding is a popular winter activity, 1990s

RAWSON HOUSE (CONT.)

It is fitting that Rawson, who is best known for his architectural contributions, held his visitation and funeral in the living room of the home he designed and loved at 2908 Forest Drive. This was not unusual for the times; many of the original homeowners in Owl's Head held their funerals in their homes rather than at a church or funeral home.

In keeping with the tradition of families living together in Owl's Head, Harvey Ingham Jr. and his family moved into 2908 Forest drive just four houses down from his parents' home at 2834 Forest Drive. Harvey Sr. and Nellie Ingham were known to pick up their grandchildren and their neighborhood friends in a chauffeur-driven limousine to enjoy a nice dinner at the downtown Des Moines Club located at 800 Locust Street.

Longtime owners John and Jane Eddy and their four children continued the tradition of making significant contributions to Des Moines. John practiced law his entire career. He was the first associate hired by Alan Whitfield in 1949 at the law firm that eventually became Whitfield & Eddy, P.L.C. He was an avid volunteer and served on several boards, including Brenton Bank, a financial institution started by Jane's family in Central Iowa. John may have been best known by his pen name, Rufus Choate, inspired by an attorney who lived in the 1800s. He used this alias when he wrote book reviews for the Des Moines Register. Jane was passionate about the home's expansive wildflower garden and spent many years cultivating it to perfection.

This home is on a one-and-a-half-acre corner lot and is situated next to a ravine at the top of a long slope. This slope has provided the perfect landscape for neighborhood children to go sledding during the long Iowa winters.

Even today groups of kids can be found bundled up with their sleds heading over to 2908 Forest Drive for some wintertime fun. The exterior is reminiscent of a traditional Cape Cod-style home with a scarlet red door beckoning passersby to give it a second look. The large stone fireplace gives off a cozy feeling that makes you want to sit under a warm blanket and sip hot chocolate. The three-season porch in the back of the home serves as a popular gathering spot due to the picturesque views it offers of the woods. The original square-patterned tile in the sun room is a reminder of Rawson's eye for quality craftsmanship. The servant quarters above the garage have had an addition, and both the kitchen and bathrooms have been remodeled over the years, but otherwise the home has maintained the vision Rawson had for his family home.

THE STAFF

Many of the Owl's Head homes were designed to accommodate live-in staff. Long-time resident Persis Gow said that in the early days of Owl's Head it was not uncommon for each home to have one or more staff members cooking and cleaning, gardening, or serving as a coachman. There was also a shared watchman position, which was responsible for the security of the neighborhood. He was expected to keep an eye out for train-hoppers from the nearby train track south of 28th Street. Over the years fewer homes had dedicated staff, and gardening and cleaning services would be shared between homes. The watchman was eventually replaced with security systems. Today most homeowners either do all of their own work or hire help as needed to maintain their residences.

In the 1940s, several residents opened their homes and sponsored Japanese-Americans from the west coast to help them avoid internment camps. It is unclear how Owl's Head residents became sponsors, although it was suspected that their affiliation with the Red Cross and Rotary Club may have facilitated the connection. One household sponsored a young Japanese woman, Chio Yamada, who helped with household duties. The rest of her family had been sent to an internment camp. Another household sponsored a couple who helped with gardening and household work. The husband of the pair, Sam Kuramoto, completed medical school while living in the neighborhood and became a prominent physician in Webster City, Iowa, until his retirement. He was known as a generous and compassionate doctor who only charged $1 for an office visit and $3 for home visits. His wife, Ayeko Kuramoto, wrote a short book about her time in Owl's Head. The Owl's Head families maintained lifelong friendships with the Japanese-Americans they sponsored.

Inside an Owl's Head home it is not uncommon to find a room designed with unique amenities for a staff member located near the back kitchen stairs or on the third floor. Some of these rooms have a separate entrance or small sink for convenience. Bells to call staff, such as butlers and house maids, were installed in many of the homes, and some had foot bells under the dining room table. The 1960s to 1980s owner of the T. M. Langan home once purchased an intriguing dragon bell at an Owl's Head yard sale. Later, while looking through old photos from the home's 1930 to 1940s owner, she saw the same bell in the dining room. She could not believe that she purchased a bell that had once belonged to the previous owners. Two years ago she returned the bell to the current owner so it could once again reside in the dining room where it had been for so many years. The bell most certainly has a special connection with the home.

Right: Coffin house, 1914. Courtesy of Drake University Archives & Special Collections

COFFIN HOUSE | 2846 FOREST DRIVE

Neighborhood lore has suggested that the "Owl's Head" name was inspired by the owl heads carved into the doorways at 2846 Forest Drive. While it's a provocative tale, the truth is likely the reverse, as the area was platted and named three years prior to construction of the home. It is likely that early owners of the land named the area after the many owls, primarily barred and great horned, that inhabit neighborhood trees.

This lavish home was built for Nathan Emery Coffin, a well-respected lawyer who co-founded the reputable law firm Dudley and Coffin with Charles Dudley. Coffin was elected to the U.S. 24th General Assembly as a Republican, but he did not seek re-election after serving his term. Coffin married Winniebel (Winnie) Belle Ewing, a member of one of Des Moines' pioneer families, in 1900 while living in the home.

Ewing's family is the namesake for Ewing Park in Des Moines. The Coffins enjoyed socializing and traveling. The Des Moines Daily News reported on a home debut party the Coffins hosted in November 1896:

"Owl's Head," the home of Mr. and Mrs. Nathan Emery Coffin, was thrown open yesterday to a large company for the first time since its completion. The occasion was an afternoon reception given by Mrs. Coffin. The exterior of this lovely home, situated in a suburban wilderness at the terminus of Forest Drive, with its picturesque architecture and quaint owl's heads, causes it to appear more like the central figure in some old romance than a modern home extending a modern hospitality. Its interior is filled as it is with those things which are pleasing to the eye and grateful to the mind, with its richly and quietly furnished apartments, and enters in a sense of perfect harmony in his surroundings. Yesterday as the ladies of the city wandered from one beautiful room to another there were continued murmurs of admiration. No color scheme was carried. Decorations of palms, roses and chrysanthemums were generously displayed throughout the apartments. A large fireplace in the front hall with leaves of palms and clusters of chrysanthemums, above which a chandelier was festooned greeted the visitors. Miss M. Carson, of Lincoln, Mrs. Nathan Coffin, Mrs. D. R. Ewing, and Mrs. H. A. Coffin constituted the receiving party. Miss Carson wore a gown of rich figured silk with a bodice of velvet, trimmed with green chiffon and carried American Beauty roses. Mrs. Coffin wore a handsome mix of dark green and brown with a vest of embroidered chiffon and mink fur trimmings.

Far Left: Coffin house dining room, 2014.

Left: Formal dinner party in the home hosted by the Lafayette Young family, 1910

COFFIN HOUSE (CONT.)

Mrs. Ewing wore black silk, with velvet trimmings. Mrs. H. A. Coffin, black silk with real trimmings. The house was illuminated with candle and gas light. In the dining room was Miss Mabel Warllold, Miss Hazelle, Miss Nettie Wyman, and Mrs. Foster Ingalls. In the cozy library Mr. and Mrs. Fred served cherry ice. Mrs. Fred wore her wedding gown of embroidered chiffon over white silk with pink sash and real trimmings. Orchestral music continued to the pleasure of the afternoon, which called out one of the most fashionably dressed companies of which Des Moines has ever boasted." *(Des Moines Daily News, November 13, 1896).*

During their travels the Coffins started purchasing art and began a small collection. Winnie set up a trust, The Coffin Fine Arts Trust, which stipulated that upon her death a museum be created to showcase both their art

collection as well as additional works purchased by the trust. The trust remains as a tribute to Winnie's late husband and continues to support and expand with important works of art at The Des Moines Art Center. [See the Artists of Owl's Head chapter for additional information].

Starting in 1906, Lafayette and Josephine Young raised their three children in this grand home they purchased from the Coffin family. Lafayette Young was a prominent politician and journalist in Iowa. He started his career in printing and founded his first weekly newspaper in 1871 -- the Atlantic Telegraph. His political career began in 1873, when he was elected to the Iowa Senate. He purchased the Des Moines Capital newspaper in 1890 and served as both editor and publisher until his death in 1926. He was a newspaper correspondent covering the First World War later in his career. He had an unsuccessful run

for Iowa governor in 1893; however, in 1894 he was elected to the office of state binder, a role responsible for binding all state publications, he held the role for six years. In 1900, he was an Iowa delegate at the Republican National Convention and nominated Theodore Roosevelt for vice president. Roosevelt and Young were personal acquaintances. There are letters from Roosevelt to Young and also from Young to Roosevelt in the collection of the Theodore Roosevelt Center at Dickinson State University. Roosevelt was also invited to the Young home in Owl's Head, but it is unclear whether or not he ever accepted the invitation. Young served in the United States Senate for four months and was a member of the Taft Commission's visit to the Philippines in 1905. Lafayette Young Jr. was president of the Greater Des Moines Committee, and according to the book Des Moines: The Pioneer of Municipal Progress

and Reform of the Middle West he played a seminal part in the new movement to boost Des Moines. The Des Moines Capital merged with the Des Moines Register in 1927 upon Young Sr.'s death.

Today, this 27-room residence remains one of Des Moines' most ornate properties. It features impressive leaded glass transoms on seven of the front and side windows, providing a rainbow of light throughout the rooms. A turret on the west side of the home and a wrap-around front porch offer an air of elegance as you approach the double-doored front entry. A fireplace greets guests as they enter the front doors, and two additional fireplaces bring warmth to the first and second floors. Some of the most memorable features of the home are the large owl talon carved into the stair railing and the owl heads that punctuate the tops of the doorways in several of the first-floor rooms. The owls and talon were carved in Germany and imported by Nathan Coffin when the home was built in early 1896. Memorable, too, is a sprawling dining room that has a glorious curved leaded glass window and a 12' built-in buffet. The room was large enough to serve forty guests a sitdown dinner for an event honoring the Danish Ambassador's visit from Chicago.

This once-grand home's sparkle had started to dim until long-time owner Rosalie Gallagher launched a major renovation in 1984. Gallagher, an interior designer, lightened the original rift sawn carved oak woodwork and wood floors. She also brightened the interior walls, ceilings, and the intricate plaster ceiling moldings. Original wall stenciling was recreated from the design found under numerous coats of paint.

Gallagher also updated the kitchen, pantry, and five bathrooms. She converted the third-floor ballroom and surrounding rooms into a design studio.

Gallagher selected an inspiring collection of Victorian colors for the outside of the home. She restored the original exterior narrow siding and the surrounding Victorian details, which had been covered with wide siding by a previous owner. Gallagher had a perennial garden planted and brought back the outside charm of the home's original setting. Her thoughtful improvements allowed it to return to a modernized version of the magnificent home the early owners intended it to be. This home has been featured in the Des Moines Register and Des Moines Homestyle, as well as in the books Victorian Architecture of Iowa and Art Work of Des Moines - Book Six.

STEVENSON HOUSE | 2834 FOREST DRIVE

The history of this grand Owl's Head gem with views overlooking Water Works Park is not entirely clear, with some accounts stating the home at 2834 Forest Drive was built in 1898 at a cost of $7,000. However, the 1903 Improvement Bulletin volume 27, a newsletter for Midwestern architects and builders, does not show a building permit being requested until 1903 for the home of Thomas and Jeannette Stevenson and their two children, Stewart and Frances. Thomas Stevenson was a Harvard-educated lawyer from Kentucky who moved to Des Moines in 1881 and started his practice near the current location of Wells Fargo Arena. He eventually became a judge in the ninth district of Des Moines and served for four years.

Famed Des Moines Register editor Harvey Ingham and his wife, Nellie, would go on to raise their three sons in this home as well. In 1909, Mr. and Mrs. Ingham joined Mr. and Mrs. Henry C. Wallace for a trip to Washington D.C. There they attended a dinner hosted by Secretary Wilson for President Theodore and First Lady Eleanor Roosevelt. Ingham became editor of the *Register* in 1927 when the *Iowa State Register* and *Des Moines Leader* newspapers consolidated. The Harvey Ingham Hall of Science at Drake University was named and dedicated in 1949, just before the honoree's death. During his time at the Register Ingham gained national acclaim, most notably for hiring famed cartoonist Ding Darling, and for the quip "write the truth, and let the chips fall where they may."

While 2834 Forest was originally built for the Stevenson family and occupied by the Ingham family, it is often referred to as "the Riley home" due to long-time owners Robert (Bob) and Mary Ann Riley. The Rileys moved into the home in the late 1940's where they raised their five children, Robert Jr. (Bob), Phil, Tim, Ben, and Ann. Like Stevenson, Bob practiced law; Mary Ann spent her career as a writer, penning reviews for both the *Iowa Daily Press* as well as the *Des Moines Register*. Later in her career, she wrote more than 400 fiction reviews for *Publisher's Weekly*. Her writing was not limited to reviews, however; she also completed nine full-length novels. Mary Ann and Bob were known for hosting social gatherings and played an integral part in events such as the annual Labor Day party, where they were staunch advocates for the party's "killer croquet tournament."

Left: Original ornate wood dining room buffet, 2020

Far Right: Chicken coup in ravine, 2020

Right: Bob and Mary Ann Riley at the Labor Day Party

STEVENSON HOUSE (CONT.)

One day in the mid-1950s, young Bob Riley Jr. decided he wanted to play baseball in his neighborhood. He trekked through the woods just west of Owl's Head with an axe as tall as he was, intending to start cutting down trees for the field. Owl's Head resident Harlan Miller of the *Des Moines Register* saw Bob on his way to the woods, and they discussed his plans to build a baseball field. Miller wrote a story about Bob's baseball plans in the *Register's* June 19, 1955 column "Over the Coffee." The story read:

I'm watching closely to see if the boys clearing the baseball diamond in our pasture will carry the project through to completion. That requires character; I think the boys have it tucked away somewhere, but occasionally they forget where they've put it.

It was not long after the article was published that the first little league park on Des Moines' west side, Racoon Valley Little League, was born. Miller clearly saw Bob's (and his pals') potential at a young age and would not be surprised to hear Bob has made a big impact on the Des Moines community ever since. The Riley family lived in the home for more than 50 years.

This elegant home is nestled next to a large ravine to the east, now home to a large community of chickens that support the current owners' neighborhood egg business. Nearby is a treehouse that overlooks the patio and ravine. A large wrap-around porch and enclosed porch on the south side of the home offer relaxing views of the ravine and neighboring homes.

A decorative fireplace is featured inside the entrance of the front door and is adorned with fleur-de-lis carvings -- a theme that is used throughout the home. The dining room features an expansive built-in buffet with original leaded glass doors. A family room, master bedroom, and screened-in porch have been added to the back of the home to extend the living space. Like many of the Owl's Head homes, the third floor was originally a ballroom that hosted parties for Des Moines' high society. It has since been converted to casual living space that is more suitable for modern accommodations. The home has been featured in *DSM magazine*.

THE NEWSPAPER PEOPLE OF OWL's HEAD

By Arnold Garson

Owl's Head was home to an enclave of top newspaper executives and journalists beginning in the late 19th century, continuing through the 20th century, that may have been unparalleled anywhere in the U.S. -- at least in terms of the concentration of newspaper firepower residing within a small neighborhood. During these years, at least one-quarter of the houses in Owl's Head were occupied -- sometimes for a few years, sometimes for a few decades -- by newspaper people.

The leadership and leading journalists from *The Des Moines Register* residing in Owl's Head included a legendary top editor of the newspaper, a Pulitzer Prize winner, reporters whose work led to highway safety and amusement ride safety reforms, a legendary columnist who helped define the morning conversation among Iowans for decades, a war correspondent who produced the first news accounts in the U.S. of what it was like to be an American prisoner of war in Vietnam, a publisher who led the newspaper through the years immediately following its designation by *Time* magazine as one of the ten best in the U.S., and a teenage copy kid who became a reporter and then rose to the rank of general counsel.

Among the personal connections boasted by the journalists of Owl's Head were U.S. presidents Abraham Lincoln and Theodore Roosevelt.

The Owl's Head newspaper story begins with two newspapers that operated in Des Moines alongside *The Register* in the late 19h century – the *Daily Iowa Capital*, later known as *The Des Moines Capital*, and the *Iowa State Leader*, later to become the *Des Moines Leader*.

W. W. Witmer was a young man attending college in Illinois in November 1863 when he decided to attend the nearby dedication of a Civil War battlefield cemetery. For the rest of his life, he would cherish the memory of having heard President Abraham Lincoln deliver the Gettysburg Address. Eight years later, after opening a law practice and operating a newspaper in Muscatine, he came to Des Moines and joined in purchasing the failed *Iowa Statesman*, to be relaunched as the *Leader*. He served as publisher and/or editor of the *Leader* until about 1882, when he turned his attention to a different area of the newspaper industry: purchasing a group of failing small-town newspapers and transforming the business into a publisher of pre-printed pages for newspapers across the Midwest. The venture, Western Newspaper Union, took off and soon had offices in major cities stretching from New York to Denver. The business was acquired in the early 1900s by

George A. Joslyn of Omaha, who would become the wealthiest man in Nebraska as he continued to grow the business. Witmer's interests moved on to real estate development, including Owl's Head and the Savery Hotel, a banking business, and a coal and mining business. He also became a power player in the Democratic Party and a fierce advocate of tariff reform. He built the house at 2900 Grand Avenue in 1903 and lived there with his family until his death in 1916. *The Leader* and the *Register* merged in 1902 when both newspapers transitioned to new ownership.

Meanwhile, Lafayette Young, a newspaperman from Atlantic, Iowa, came to Des Moines in 1890 and bought *The Capital*. He built the house at 2848 Forest Drive the following year. Young served as publisher and editor of *The Capital* until his death in 1926. His death was followed five weeks later by that of his wife, Josephine, who had run the newspaper when Lafayette went to Cuba in 1898 to cover the Spanish-American War. There he had met Theodore Roosevelt, commander of the Rough Riders, and the two men became close friends. Two years later, Young placed Roosevelt's name in nomination for vice president of the United States at the Republican National Convention, a nomination that gave Roosevelt the presidency when William McKinley was assassinated in 1901.

Left: Harvey Ingham in his Des Moines Register office on his sixtieth anniversary of being a news editor. Courtesy of Iowa State University Press

Young covered two more wars for his newspaper – the Second Balkan War in southeastern Europe in 1913 and World War I in 1915, before the U.S. entered that war. He also served five months as a U.S. Senator in 1910 to 1911, as he was appointed to fill a vacant seat. In 1927, within a year of the Youngs' deaths, *The Capital*, an afternoon paper, was sold to The Register and Tribune Co. and consolidated with the *Tribune*.

The *Register's* first connection with Owl's Head dates to a little more than 100 years ago, when Harvey Ingham and his family acquired the house at 2834 Forest Drive, two doors east of Lafayette Young. Ingham had come to Des Moines from Algona as associate editor of *The Register and Leader* in 1902, and persuaded his banker friend, Gardner Cowles, also of Algona, to join him in Des Moines and buy the newspaper the following year. For the next 40 years, the two men worked together, Ingham as editor, Cowles as publisher, shaping a statewide newspaper of national renown. *The Register*, as it was known beginning in 1915, won its first four Pulitzer Prizes – two for Ding Darling in editorial cartooning and two for editorial writing – under Ingham's leadership. Ingham lived at 2834 Forest Drive until his death in 1949. His son William Ingham, a lawyer, lived nearby at 2908 Forest Drive in the 1930s and 40s.

After the Inghams, 2834 Forest became the home of Mary Ann Riley and her family. Riley was a freelance writer who authored about 400 book reviews and nine novels. Her book reviews were a fixture on *The Register's* book page. Books were central to the lives of both Riley and of Ingham, who was a passionate book collector. Ingham donated his collection of about 500 rare books, including a first edition of Dr. Samuel Johnson's dictionary, to Drake University.

In 1931 or 1932, Harlan Miller and his family became Owl's Head residents at 2900 Forest Drive, where they remained for more than 30 years. Miller created the daily "Over the Coffee" column in *The Register* in 1925 and wrote it until his retirement in 1968, with time out for service in World War II. The column was, as his successor Donald Kaul described it, a collection of anecdotes, jokes, and pithy observations – and it captivated Iowans each morning for decades. Miller and his family remained Owl's Head residents until the mid-to-late 1960s.

Gordon Gammack and his family became Owl's Head residents around 1946, about 13 years after he joined *The Register and Tribune* news staff. Gammack, also a daily columnist, lived at 2800 Forest Drive until his death in 1974. He memorably covered three wars: World War II, the Korean War, and Vietnam. His column appeared in the afternoon *Des Moines Tribune*, where it became a fixture on Page 1. His report about the experiences of Iowan Michael Kjome, a POW held by the North Vietnamese for five years, won one of the nation's top journalism awards in 1974: the National Headliner Award. Gordon's daughter, Julie Gammack, purchased the house on Forest from her mother and lived there from 1986 to 1989; she, too, worked for *The Register* as a columnist (1984 to 1992).

James McGuire came to work for The Register as assistant farm editor in 1950. He and his family resided at 2831 Ridge Road beginning in 1955. He progressed in his career to farm editor and then editor of the "Farm and Home" section in *The Register*. As farm editor he wrote a series of articles about the dangers of slow-moving farm vehicles, which resulted in legislation creating the fluorescent orange warning triangles that still appear on combines and tractors as they drive the state's roads today. The McGuires remained at 2831 until a few years after he retired in 1981.

Frank Miller joined *The Register* in 1953, and his editorial cartoons appeared daily on Page 1 until his death in 1983. He won the Pulitzer Prize for editorial cartooning in 1963. He and his family resided at 2848 Ridge Road from 1965 until about 1974. Frank's work as a scenic watercolorist also is widely known and respected. His daughter, Mindy, who grew up at 2848 Ridge, worked at The Register as an artist in the news department. [See the Artists of Owl's Head chapter for additional information on Frank Miller].

Charles C. Edwards, Jr., the grandson of Gardner Cowles, was president and publisher of The Register for several years beginning in 1985. Edwards and his wife lived at 2833 Forest Drive in the mid-1980s. He served as the newspaper's top executive through the time following its recognition as one of the nation's 10 best newspapers and through its transition to new ownership in 1985.

Barbara Mack started working at *The Register* as a teenage copy courier in the late 1960s. She studied journalism at Iowa State University and continued at The Register as an intern, a staff reporter, and a food critic. After earning a law degree at Drake University, she joined *The Register's* legal department, ultimately becoming corporation secretary and general counsel. After *The Register* was sold to Gannett in 1985, she turned to teaching journalism and media law at Iowa State. She and her husband purchased the house at 305 28th Street in 1989 and resided there until 2006, with Barbara hosting countless gatherings of her journalism students and the women of The Register's news staff in her Owl's Head home during those years. Barbara died in 2012.

My family and I lived at 2815 Ridge Road from 1976 to 1989. I worked for the Des Moines Tribune and then The Register from 1969 to 1989. My coverage of a fatal roller coaster accident in Arnold's Park, Iowa, in the 1970s led to the state's first amusement ride inspection and safety law. Later I was an investigative reporter and then managing editor of The Register; the latter provided the opportunity to oversee two Pulitzer Prize-winning projects. There wasn't a better job in newspapering or a better neighborhood in which to live. Also, unknowingly taking a cue from what might be called the "house of books" at 2834 Forest, I began specialized book-collecting during our time in Owl's Head: first, old dictionaries, then children's fiction relating to newspapers.

Speaking of 2834 Forest, the connection of that house to newspapers was continuous for more than eight decades, the longest span of any house in Owl's Head. Mary Ann Riley continued to reside there until 2004; her last book review for *The Register* appeared in 2001, but she wrote book reviews for other publications until 2007, two years before her death at age 90.

Above: Gordon Gammack on location in Vietnam, 1970

GILCREST HOUSE | 2814 FOREST DRIVE

Despite the numerous Gilcrest family members who resided in Owl's Head for much of their lives, the home at 2814 Forest Drive remains the seminal Gilcrest home. This home, affectionately known as "The Gilcrest House" was built for siblings Charles, Caroline, and Belle Gilcrest. The original lot was purchased by Gilcrest Lumber Company in 1904, and the home was completed a year later at a total cost of just over $12,000. It was designed by architect H. D. Rawson, who designed and built his own family's home just down the street. The builder was Gilcrest Lumber Company, the company founded by the two older siblings of the original owners, J. K. and W. H. Gilcrest.

Members of the Gilcrest family built two other homes in Owl's Head: at 2800 Forest Drive and 415 28th Street, both designed by C. C. Cross and Sons. The house at 2800 Forest Drive was built in 1905 for Caroline Lichty, the niece of Charles, Caroline, and Belle Gilcrest, and shared a communal garage that was located behind 2814 Forest Drive. The Lichty family resided in the home from 1905 until 1944, when the rights to the garage were given solely to 2814. The carriage house was converted to a home in 1961. The Gammack family purchased 2800 Forest Drive in 1944 and lived there for many years. Gordon Gammack was a renowned columnist and reporter for the *Des Moines Register* covering World War II, the Korean War, and the Vietnam War. [See the Newspaper People of Owl's Head for additional information]. The home at 415 28th Street was a gift from the Gilcrest Company to J. S. Gilcrest and his bride, who lived there until her death in 1933. Members of the Gilcrest family inherited the home and continued to reside at 415 28th Street until it was sold in 1948.

GILCREST HOUSE (CONT.)

Given the backing of the Gilcrest Lumber Company, it comes as no surprise that the home is appointed with the highest quality materials. The interior wood and hardware were imported from Europe and were assembled by the best craftsmen working in Des Moines at the time. The home was equipped with both gas jets and electrical lighting and also included a central vacuum system in the original design. Additional technological advances in the home were a built-in intercom system with whistles to attract attention, a third-floor water reservoir that fed the emergency fire system, and a cistern that allowed servants to wash clothes using rainwater. Rawson included drawings for some of the woodwork and glass art features. Former owner Gregor Gentleman described the stained glass art as "somewhat reminiscent of the type of work being done by Frank Lloyd Wright at the same time in Oak Park and Riverside, Illinois."

The most notable art glass is a large feature in the stairway between the second and third floors. The wood veneers are ¼-inch thick, and the exterior walls are constructed with three air spaces. Prominent front pillars create a stately entrance to the medieval rectilinear style home. The Gilcrest family clearly valued quality and innovation.

Caroline Gilcrest's untimely death in late 1906 only allowed her a little more than a year in the home. Her estate was passed on to her siblings who resided with her. Her brother, Charles, lived there until 1922 at which time Belle became the sole owner. Belle resided there for 46 years until 1951 when she was 94 years old. Her niece and next door neighbor, Caroline Lichty, had moved into 2814 to care for Belle until her death and ultimately inherited the home. She lived there until 1958. Large old homes were not in high demand in 1958, and Caroline sold the home for a mere $18,000, only $6,000 more than the cost to build it nearly six decades earlier.

Gregor and Julia Gentleman moved into the home in 1958. The home was in good condition and only required varnish removed and rewiring to prepare it for the next long-term residents. In 1960, Gregor started his affectionately-named business, Owl's Head Engineering Company, in the former maid's quarters in the northwest corner of the second floor. He expanded into the basement within a year. Not long after he acquired his first company and changed the company name to "Swanson Gentleman Inc.," the company grew to acquire 37 companies throughout the Midwest. His businesses sold many of the products once sold by Gilcrest Lumber Company.

Like her great-grandfather and great-great-grandfather who served as Iowa senators, Julia Gentleman served as a Republican in the Iowa House of Representatives from 1975 until 1977 and in the Iowa Senate from 1979 to 1989. The Gentlemans raised three daughters and two sons at 2814 Forest Drive. They owned the home until 2005.

Recent owners have carefully renovated and maintained the home, allowing it to remain the grand vision initially conceived by both Rawson and the Gilcrest family.

Above: Original architect's rendering of the Gilcrest house completed by Hallett & Rawson Architects, ca. 1904

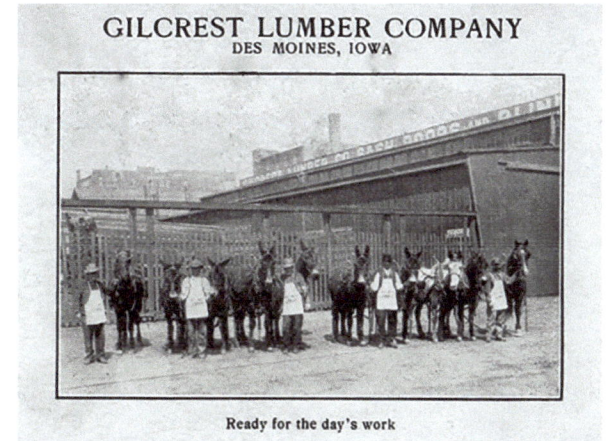

GILCREST LUMBER COMPANY
DES MOINES, IOWA

Ready for the day's work

THE GILCREST LUMBER COMPANY

The Gilcrest Lumber Company was founded in 1856 by J. K. and W. H. Gilcrest and headquartered in Des Moines. It was the first lumber mill in Des Moines. Gilcrest Lumber Company built its reputation on superior customer service and top-quality building materials. In addition to J. K. and W. H. Gilcrest, younger siblings Charles, Caroline, Belle, and Anne Marie Lichty (Caroline's mother) were stockholders in the company.

The Gilcrest Lumber Company was founded at a time when trees were much more plentiful in Iowa. New settlers trying to develop family farms were willing to part with trees on their land for a low price. Oxen and mules were used to transport the lumber to the mills. Rafts were built when river transportation was required. When the Gilcrest houses on Forest Drive were built, the company transformed lumber into doors, sashes, shingles, milled flooring, lumber, and lath. They also distributed items often found in home improvement stores such as nails, paint, glass for windows, and builders hardware. These goods were initially delivered to customers by mules and eventually replaced by white Gilcrest trucks. As part of their commitment to superior customer service, deliveries were always free.

John Gilcrest, of 415 28th Street, worked for his father at Gilcrest Lumber. Despite the family's focus on lumber, John experimented with incubators. He created innovative features for the incubator and started a profitable mail-order business six years after his Owl's Head home was built in 1898. He went on to achieve world-wide acclaim for his egg incubators and helped increase both the efficiency and productivity of the poultry industry.

The company continued to be run by Gilcrest family members until the company merged with Des Moines competitor Jewett Companies to form Gilcrest/Jewett Lumber Company in late 1985. The two companies' bond had started before the merger, when they helped each other persevere after each experienced detrimental fires at their facilities. Today the joint company is headquartered in Waukee, Iowa, and maintains three other locations across the state: in Altoona, Marion, and Coralville.

The Gilcrest Lumber Company has stood the test of time and remains the oldest firm of any kind in Des Moines – as well as the oldest retail lumber company under one family ownership west of the Mississippi River.

BRECHT HOUSE | 2829 FOREST DRIVE

One of the first residential dwellings constructed near downtown Des Moines was the elegant 2829 Forest Drive, built in 1890. With the completion of the Des Moines-based State Capitol in 1886, this land became prime real estate, with views of the Capitol and of beautiful Water Works Park. The area around the home and its idyllic setting would soon become what we celebrate today as Owl's Head.

The home was designed in Rectilinear Queen Anne style, which was considered by many to be the most fashionable in home design from 1880 to 1905. Queen Anne design was the culmination of the Romantic period and was a combination of various forms and stylistic features borrowed from earlier parts of the Victorian and Romantic eras. Noted characteristics include steeply pitched roofs, irregular roof shapes, a dominant front-facing gable, patterned shingles, bay windows, and multiple gables and dormers.

The double-wide lot at 2829 Forest Drive was considered an extravagance, even in this upscale neighborhood. The narrow driveway, designed for horse and carriage, has welcomed homeowners and their guests up the hill for 130 years. It is not by coincidence that the driveway has always been made of brick. The original owner, William Brecht, was a prominent businessman and in 1888 held the position of superintendent of Des Moines Brick Manufacturing Company. Five years later in 1893, Brecht formed his own successful company, Flint Brick Company.

A leader in a thriving Des Moines industry, Brecht and his wife, Johanna, helped shape the Owl's Head neighborhood and its place in Des Moines high society. One can picture Mr. and Mrs. Brecht as they departed their grand home for a social event by horse-drawn carriage. They would have, of course, likely been wearing the latest in fashion: a floor length tulip bell skirt for the Mrs., and for Mr. Brecht a tailored and fitted wool suit with tie.

In 1895 the home was sold to Marcus Younker, one of the three founding brothers of Younker & Bros., a dry goods store that originally opened in Keokuk, Iowa, in 1856. It was Marcus' half-brother Herman who owned and was president of the store that became the upscale Younkers department store chain. After the store in Keokuk closed, Marcus moved to Des Moines and worked for Herman until his retirement in 1895. The store was family-owned until 1923, when it was sold to J. Mandelbaum & Sons. The Younkers name, however, remained until its closing in 2018 after 162 years in business.

The mortgage for the home was listed as $980 in 1890 when William and Johanna Brecht made the original purchase. The Brechts sold the house to Marcus Younker for $2,000 under contract for deed in 1893. Marcus defaulted on the loan in 1895 and in 1896 the Brechts foreclosed on Marcus. On that same day in 1896, the house was sold to Herman Younker, the half-brother of Marcus, for $3,000.

Two of Iowa's greatest 20th-century artists, Jules Kirschenbaum and his wife, Cornelis Ruhtenberg, moved to Des Moines in 1963 when Kirschenbaum assumed the position of artist-in-residence at the Des Moines Art Center. In 1967 the Bronx, N.Y., native was offered the position of principal painting instructor at Drake University, where he continued to work for the remainder of his life.

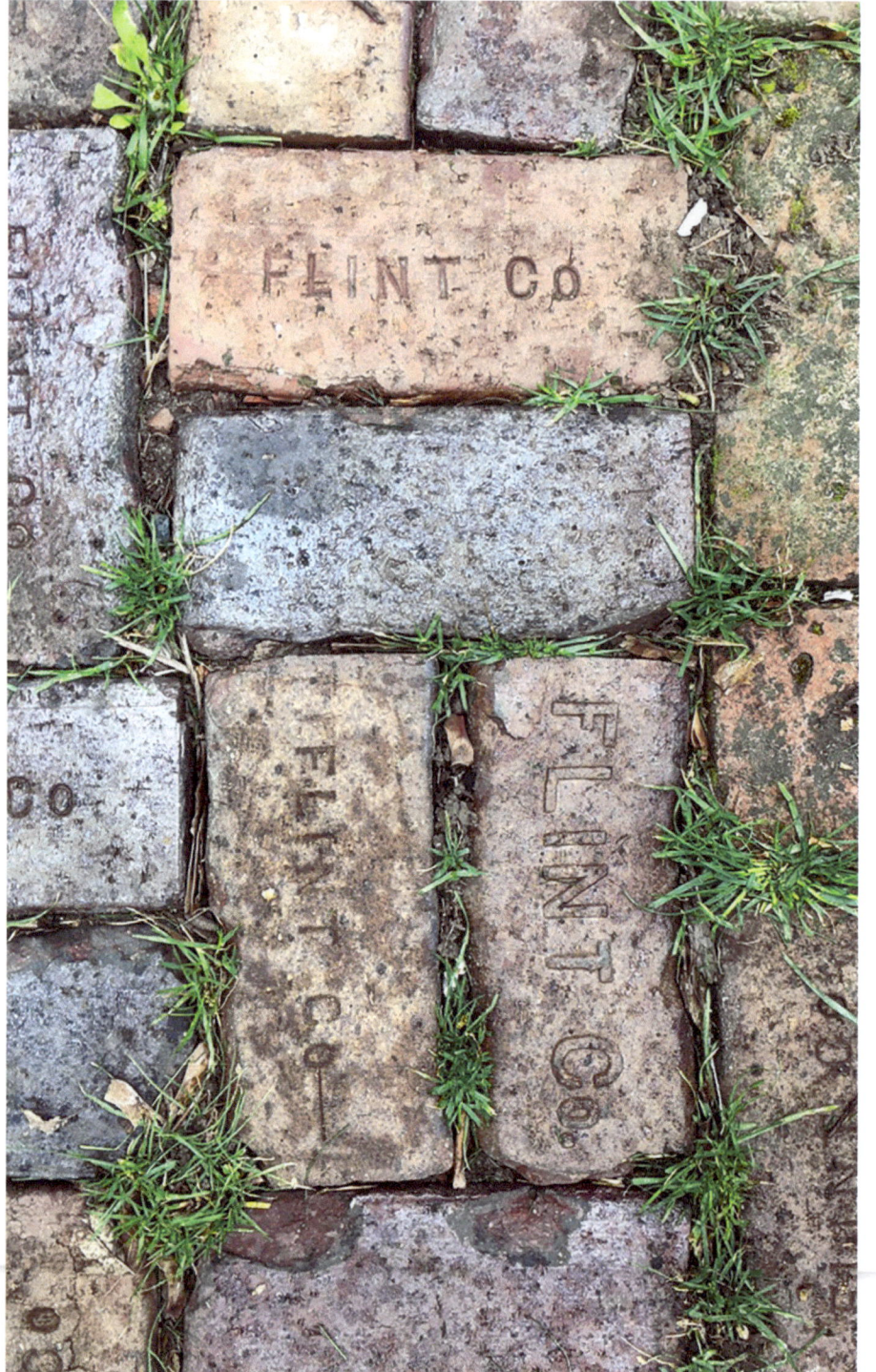

BRECHT HOUSE (CONT.)

Kirschenbaum and Ruhtenberg lived in Owl's Head for more than 40 years and raised their son, Matthew, there. Jules Kirschenbaum used his home studio as a backdrop for numerous compositions. Distinct evidence of this can be seen in Studio I, 1976-78 and in Studio with Mirror, 1984, in which he includes precise home interior details such as a window location, wood floor and base details, door handle design, and electrical outlet locations. An easel, believed to have been used by Kirschenbaum, has been sold as a permanent fixture with the home. [See Artists of Owl's Head chapter for additional information on Jules Kirschenbaum.]

Ruhtenberg, a painter as well as professional flutist, was born in Riga, Latvia in 1923. As with Kirschenbaum, she was well-known in the national art community. Her first New York exhibition early in her career was met with great success. [See Artists of Owl's Head chapter for additional information on Cornelis Ruhtenberg.]

Previous owner Nicole Lozier, who lived at 2829 Forest Drive with husband John and their 3 children from 2013 to 2018, recalls a story about hiring a man to grind out the stump after they lost a front-yard tree:

"I came out the front door when he arrived, and he looked up at me with a very familiar look on his face as if he knew me. I didn't recognize him and asked if I knew him. He replied with a sweet smile of remembrance that he didn't know me but that he 'grew up' in the house. He said he was the best friend of Kirschenbaum and Ruhtenberg's son, and spent a lot of time in the house. I invited him in, and he proceeded to tell me all about the home - much of which was based upon the artwork they had and where they had it hung. He remembered that the Kirschenbaum house was 'something special and almost magical . . . the house always had nice music playing and books everywhere . . . it always felt like you were at home in a special place.'"

ARTISTS OF OWL'S HEAD

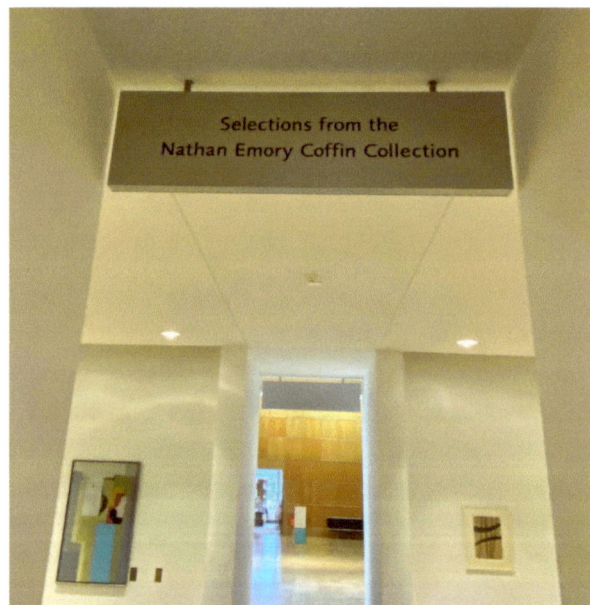

Above: *Nathan Emory Coffin art collection at the Des Moines Art Center, 2021*

Right: *Des Moines Art Center, 2021*

Far Right: *A bronze plaque in the Des Moines Art Center commemorates the gifts given by Nathan Emory Coffin*

With a major donor to the Des Moines Art Center having lived in Owl's Head, it is only fitting that the neighborhood would also be home to a number of artists who have had an impact on the national art scene. From paintings to cartoons, wood carving to lithography, paper cutting, mosaic work, and illustrations, there is a rich and diverse history of art that has been created in Owl's Head studios.

COFFIN FAMILY
2846 FOREST DRIVE

The Des Moines Art Center got tremendous support from a family who lived in Owl's Head. Nathan Emory and Winniebel (Ewing) Coffin, who were the first owners at 2846 Forest Drive, gave the Des Moines Art Center its first trust: The Coffin Fine Arts Trust. Nathan Emory Coffin was the son of H.A. Coffin, who formed the Iowa Loan and Trust Company. An 1885 graduate of Harvard Law School, Nathan taught at Drake Law School for many years and was a member of the Drake Board of Trustees. He served in the Iowa legislature in 1890. [See Coffin House chapter for additional information on the Coffin Family].

NATHAN EMORY COFFIN COLLECTION
IN MEMORY OF
NATHAN EMORY COFFIN
BORN IN ALLEGHENY CITY, PENNSYLVANIA
FEBRUARY 2ND, 1863
DIED AT DES MOINES, IOWA
JANUARY 30TH, 1931

Far Right: Pyrography on the fireplace at the master bedroom of 331 28th Street created by Fay Atkins Weaver, 2020

Right: Fay Atkins Weaver in front of her home at 331 28th Street, early 1900s

PERSIS WEAVER ROBERTSON AND FAY ATKINS WEAVER
331 28TH STREET

Persis (Robertson) Gow, who was instrumental in providing information for this book, passed in March 2020 at age 94. Her mother, Persis (Weaver) Robertson, studied lithography at the Stone City Art Colony under Lowell Houser and Adrian Dornbush. The art colony, having been formed by Edward Rowan, Adrian Dornbush, and Grant Wood, existed during the summers of 1932 and 1933 on the John A. Green Estate in Stone City, Iowa.

Robertson gradually moved away from lithography and took up paper cutting as a creative outlet later on in life. She showed her work in group exhibitions at numerous locations, including the Art Institute of Chicago, the Library of Congress, the Corcoran Gallery, the Philadelphia Print Club, the Brooklyn Museum, and the Pennsylvania Academy of Fine Arts. While living in Des Moines, she submitted art to the Iowa State Fair and often won prizes. She and her husband, Albert Robertson, were on the planning committee for the Des Moines Art Center. One of her lithographs entitled Front Door is owned by the Smithsonian American Art Museum.

Persis Gow's grandmother, Fay Atkins Weaver, and husband James built the house at 331 28th Street. Fay studied at the Cummings School of Art, and throughout the years, received continued training in wood carving and pyrography (a burning technique she used to create designs on wood surfaces). Fay designed and created many of the ornate details still found in the home, including pyrography on beams and around the fireplaces, and custom-built furniture. Weaver used her pyrography skills to create astrological signs around the master bedroom fireplace and was the mastermind behind the dragon carvings, seashell doorway, and other ornate details on the outside of the home. [See the Atkins Weaver House chapter for additional information on the Weaver Family].

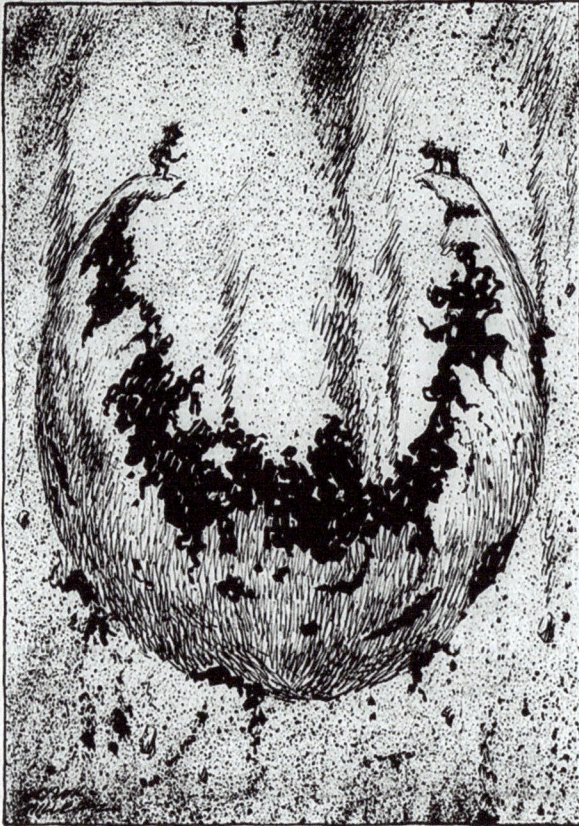

"I SAID — WE SURE SETTLED THAT DISPUTE, DIDN'T WE!"

Left: Frank Miller's Pulitzer Prize-winning cartoon, 1964

Below Left: Frank Miller's sketch of 2834 Forest Drive

FRANK MILLER
2848 RIDGE ROAD

Frank Andrea Miller was a cartoonist for the Des Moines Register from 1953 to 1983. He was recommended for the job by his former teacher, Karl Mattern, who was a contemporary of Grant Wood. Over the course of his 30-year career, he created more than 10,000 cartoons. His caricatures and cartoons responded to politics and the human condition. At the time of his death, his cartoons were syndicated in nearly 50 newspapers nationally. He won a Pulitzer Prize in editorial cartooning for a cartoon on nuclear warfare in 1964. Miller was also an accomplished watercolorist, mostly painting scenes featuring rural towns, vintage buildings, and picturesque farms.

When the Millers sold their home in the mid-1970s, they reportedly sold stacks of his original drawings at a garage sale for 25 cents each. His wife, Kathryn Miller, who met Frank at the Kansas City Art Institute, worked as a fashion illustrator early in her career and later worked in batik. Daughters Melissa and Melinda (Mindy) are both artists: Melissa works in Pique Assiette Mosaics while Mindy, like her father, worked for the Des Moines Register early in her career. Frank Miller, Sr., Frank's father, had been an illustrator for the Kansas City Star for 40 years. [See the Newspaper People of Owl's Head chapter for additional information on Frank Miller].

Right: Jules Kirschenbaum's final portrait of Robert Riley, Sr.

Below Right: Jules Kirschenbaum sketch of Robert Riley, Sr.

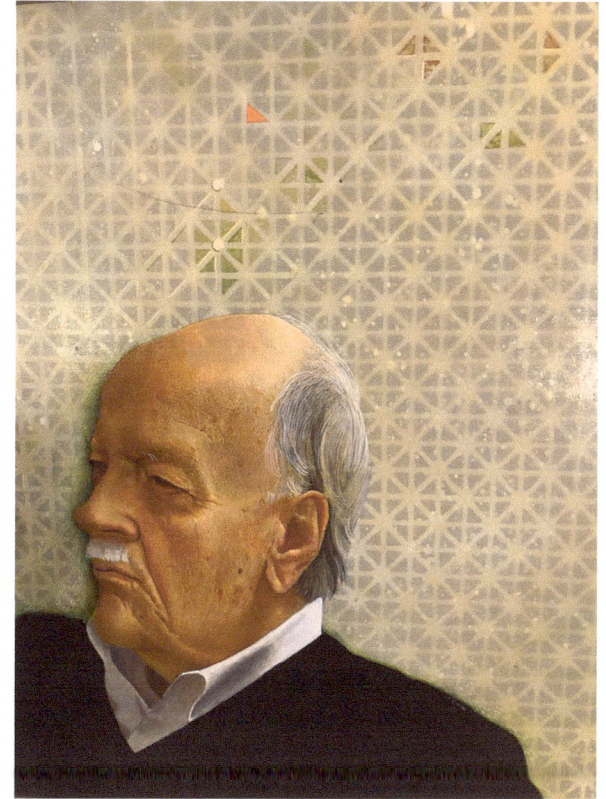

JULES KIRSCHENBAUM
2829 FOREST DRIVE

Jules Kirschenbaum originally began his studies in figurative work. Later, refining his art, he moved away from his early figurative Renaissance-inspired style. He then began experimenting with abstraction, only to return to realism. Taking another turn, Kirschenbaum began a period in which his art was considered part of the "magic realism" movement. Finally, he entered a period of creating art about meaning and about the "meaning of meaning." According to Gandelman in Visible Language XXIII 2/3, Kirschenbaum stated, "One contemporary concept is 'what you see is what you see.' In contrast to that, I am for an art in which what you see is only the beginning of an endless chain of illusions . . ." (p. 299).

Kirschenbaum painted in multiple mediums, such as tempera, oil, acrylic, and gouache. Influenced by surrealism and often dealing with the subject of mortality, he frequently repeated motifs such as self-portraits, bones, inscriptions, and elaborate detailing. Kirschenbaums's art can be seen at the Metropolitan Museum of Art, Des Moines Art Center, Hirshhorn Museum, National Academy of Design, Sheldon Memorial Art Gallery, the University of Iowa Stanley Museum of Art, and Butler Institute of American Art. [See Brecht House chapter for additional information on Jules Kirschenbaum].

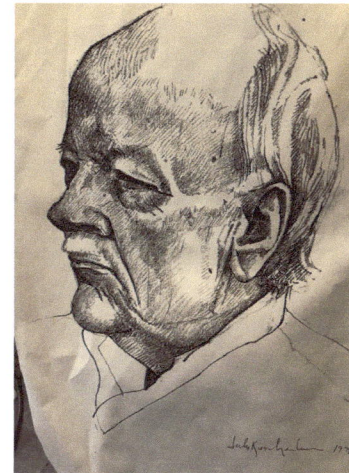

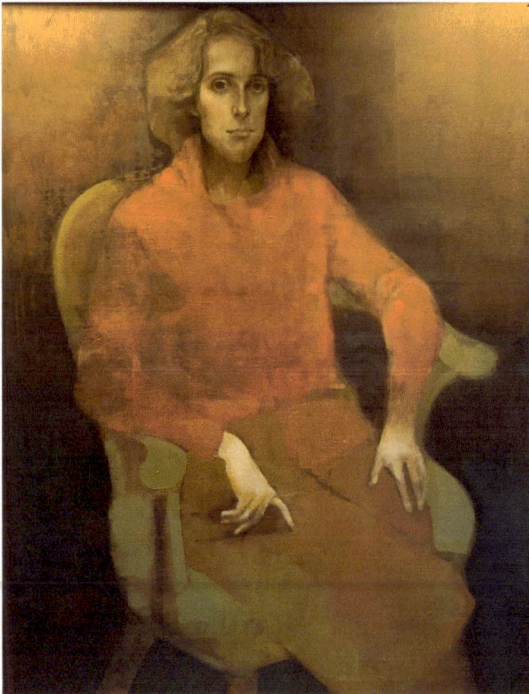

Above Left: Cornelis Ruhtenberg's portrait of Mary Ann Riley

Below Left: Cornelis Ruhtenberg's portrait of Kay Riley

CORNELIS RUHTENBERG
2829 FOREST DRIVE

Cornelis Ruhtenberg's art is mostly figurative and was based upon getting to know her subjects intuitively to understand their essence; she was not interested in duplicating reality. Her expressionistic style included using shapes and varying color tones to evoke a mood. Her work has been exhibited at numerous locations, some of which include: Forum Gallery, MoMA, Metropolitan Museum of Art, National Academy, Smithsonian American Art Museum, Hirshhorn Museum, National Institute of Arts and Letters, Corcoran Gallery, Chicago Art Institute, Denver Art Museum, Pennsylvania Academy of Fine Arts, and Berlin Museum. [See Brecht House chapter for additional information on Cornelis Ruhtenberg].

Far Right above and below: Sarah Grant's abstract art

Right: Sticks art

SARAH GRANT
2804 RIDGE ROAD

Sarah Grant grew up in Ames, Iowa and earned her BFA, MA, and MFA at the University of Iowa. Her conceptual painting style is rooted in Abstract Expressionism and its two schools within the movement: narrative and non-narrative. She has recently been "focusing on large-scale oil paintings to push and expand her understanding of abstraction as it relates to storytelling." Installations include Des Moines Art Center, Prairie Meadows, Principal Life Insurance, Ruan Center, and Security National Bank. Grant, who lives in Des Moines, currently shows her work at the Moberg Gallery.

The Sticks brand, founded in 1986, is based upon Grant's hand-drawn imagery on wood. Her Sticks art has a lighthearted, life-affirming flavor and philosophy. Sticks is nationally known for its distinctive line of furniture, accessories, and object art. Installations include Iowa State University, Blank Children's Hospital, Urbandale Public Library, and Grand Rapids, Michigan. Sticks products can be purchased online at https://sticks.com or in stores nationally. [See Reynolds House chapter for additional information on Sarah Grant].

Fortunately, art by several of the artists listed above is owned by current and former Owl's Head residents. Additional work by these artists can be found online.

Far Right: Watt house, 1990s

Right: Prized dark bay stallion, Hail Cloud, owned by James Watt

WATT HOUSE | 313 28TH STREET

The land on which 313 28th Street stands was part of Polk & Hubbell Park before it was sold for single-family homes. Frederick M. Hubbell, second owner of the nearby mansion that is now the governor's mansion, Terrace Hill, sold the lot to James and Mary Watt in 1885. James Watt had made an impressive climb professionally from a laborer to the president of both the German Savings Bank and The Humane Society. The Watts commissioned the construction of the home, one of the original built in Craftsman style in Owl's Head, and included a barn and a small pasture likely used for the fine horses James was a pioneer in breeding and racing. His most prized horse, Hail Cloud, clocked an impressive time of 2:07 ¾ in the mile race and later became the oldest standardbred horse in the United States. James Watt left a trust fund for Hail Cloud in his will ensuring the horse received proper care until he died. The barn has since been converted into a single-family home and sold separately.

The land for the pasture was also sold, and a single-family home has since been built on the property. Tales of an underground tunnel connecting the house and barn, giving James access to his beloved horses, have been passed down by owners. For many years it was referred to as "The White House" due to its exterior white color; however, in the last 20 years it has been painted both green and dark gray and the name has been retired.

Longtime owner George Moore was an obstetrician whose life was marked by controversial twists and turns. He had his own private practice on Ingersoll Avenue and had previously been chairman of neurology and pathology at Still College of Osteopathy. He purchased the home with his wife, Lillie, in 1906, and they raised their son and daughter, Kenneth and Florence, there. Moore, however, started an affair with one of his Owl's Head neighbors. While it is unclear if the affair was the reason,

the Moores divorced in 1919. Lillie continued to live in the home until her death in 1936. Dr. Moore remarried and purchased a home nearby on 29th Street in Owl's Head.

In 1938, Dr. Moore was charged with second-degree murder and accused of performing an illegal abortion on a 17-year-old girl, Velda Mass, that resulted in the girl's death. The case was highly publicized locally, with Dr. Moore insisting that Mass came to his practice to treat appendicitis when he determined she was having a miscarriage and gave her heat therapy treatment. The baby's father argued that he dropped Mass off at Dr. Moore's office with money for an illegal abortion several days before her death. Although her autopsy showed that her cause of death was septic peritonitis due to an illegal operation, a jury consisting of all women found George Moore not guilty. He continued to practice medicine until his retirement in 1962.

Above Left: Hand-carved custom bracket at the front entry pocket doors, 2020

Above Middle: View of original interior doors and stained glass, 2020

Above Right: William Morris wallpaper in the front entry, thought to be original to the home, 2020

WATT HOUSE (CONT.)

The home had been an important location for young women during both World Wars I and II. In 1917, the Girls Volunteer Aids, a group whose mission was to entertain enlisted men by organizing social events such as dances and luncheons in the community, held their first event there. The girls were forbidden from dating the men who attended these events. Florence Moore was a member of the organization. They served a picnic supper to 25 enlisted men from Camp Dodge. The event's success ignited the planning of more events for soldiers, many at a much grander scale. During World War II the home was transformed into a multi-resident home for young women. Most of the women were living there while waiting for their significant others to return from the war. Parties were held when the men returned. Tenants rented private bedrooms and shared common areas of the home such as the living and dining rooms.

Longtime owners of nearly 50 years, the Winnies, owned the popular family-style restaurant, Sherry's, located on Ingersoll Avenue not far from Dr. Moore's office, until it closed in 1973. The Winnies converted two sections of the home into apartments. Ultimately, the home was converted back to a single-family residence

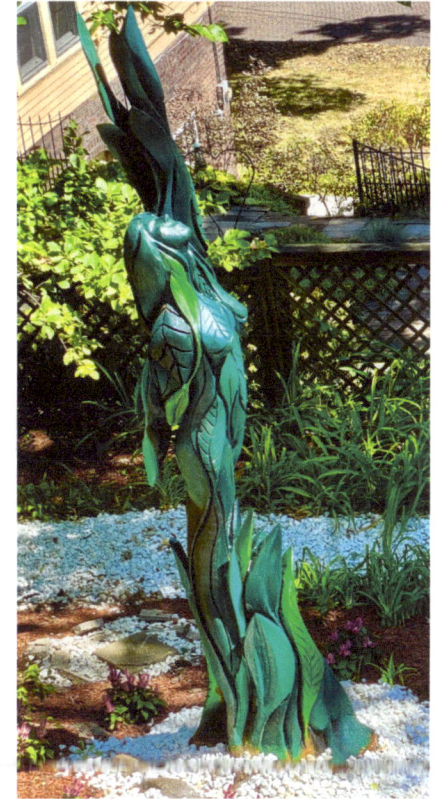

when purchased by renovators Richard and Carroll Michalek in 1990. It remains a single-family home today. Carroll Michalek's aunt was long-time resident Jane Eddy of 2908 Forest Drive and may have influenced the Michaleks' choice of neighborhoods.

This home has a prominent front porch accented with expansive gardens. Quilts were displayed in the gardens as a feature for the 2011 book Utility Quilting: Simple Solutions for Quick Hand Quilting by Carolyn Forster. A new addition to the garden is a Nature figure, designed by Gary Keenan, rendered from an old tree stump. The figure has been appropriately named "Derecha" after the hurricane-like derecho that swept through Iowa in August 2020 just as Keenan started work on the figure. Derecha's tree stump survived the storm, but a large tree and much of the yard suffered severe damage as a result of the unusual weather event.

Given its impressive size, the house was often used for entertaining and includes French doors that open from the dining room to the porch to provide guests with more room to socialize. As they continue to explore beyond the front door, guests experience more French doors, as well as pocket doors, with colorful stained-glass windows. The front entryway has greeted visitors with original William Morris "Iris" wallpaper over the years, and the back stairway leads to the most memorable room in the home: the master bedroom. The room is surrounded by windows of all shapes and sizes with views of Water Works Park and Gray's Lake.

"

I may be out there for only six months.
Of course I hope it doesn't turn out that way,
but you never can tell.

AN UNLIKELY NEIGHBOR

During the mid-1930's when Dr. George Moore would have been walking home from his practice at Ingersoll Avenue on a daily basis, he would likely have passed by the apartment buildings on Grand Ave. and 28th Street in Des Moines, where a young radio sports announcer was renting an apartment.

At the same time, Dite (Dwight) Myers, his brother Hi, and his sister Tine formed a friendship with this new young sports announcer, and future U.S. President Ronald Reagan, who was working at WHO Radio. The Myers siblings spent many evenings together with Reagan in the 1930s at the Moonlight Inn, a speakeasy at 73rd and University in Clive, Iowa. This friendship would last more than 50 years. While at WHO, Reagan made a name for himself by creating play-by-play accounts of Chicago Cubs baseball games using only the basic descriptions the station received by wire as the games were in progress. During the years from 1934 to 1937 the Chicago Cubs were successful in the National League and earned a spot in the 1935 World Series, giving Reagan even more publicity as a sports announcer. [See A Musical Guest chapter for Myers Family connections to Owl's Head].

While covering the Cubs in Los Angeles in 1937, Reagan met with American singer and actress Joy Hodges, a Des Moines native then working in the movies, and told her he would like to get into "pictures." Hodges set up a screen test, and by the time Reagan returned back to Des Moines, he had a contract with Warner Brothers. A 1937 Des Moines Tribune article quotes Reagan as saying: "I may be out there for only six months. Of course I hope it doesn't turn out that way, but you never can tell."

Reagan, of course, would go on to become the 40th President of the United States. Hodges and Reagan remained friends for over 60 years, and she was a frequent guest at the White House during his presidency.

Another favorite summer hangout for Reagan while he lived in Des Moines was the Camp Dodge pool in Johnston, Iowa. As a former lifeguard, he enjoyed spending his days in the sun. It has been said that he rescued one or two swimmers there.

Reagan lived in a few different places during his time in Des Moines, most notably the brick apartment buildings located at the northwest corner of Grand Avenue and 28th Street, adjacent to Owl's Head. These apartment buildings exist today and are slated for a $8.3 million renovation. The complex will be renamed Reagan House and is expected to open in spring 2022. At the time of this writing, there is a movement to place Reagan House on the National Register of Historic Places.

Bill Peverill, nephew to Dite, Hi, and Tine Myers, recalled his family moving from Des Moines to Hollywoodland in Los Angeles for about two years when he was a child. Peverill had fond memories of the day a nice family friend named Ronald Reagan came to babysit for Peverill. Reagan was 27 years old at the time and Peverill was 9. [See A Musical Guest chapter for more Peverill Family connections to Owl's Head].

A story recalled by Ben Guise, a Des Moines area resident, states that when Reagan was being interviewed for a radio show at the age of 80, after eight years of living in the White House, he was asked about the time he lived in Des Moines as a sports announcer. Reagan fondly recalled spending many evenings listening to music at the Moonlight Inn and noted that one of his most prized possessions was a sign from the Inn. The original sign had been gifted to him by an old friend he had known from years earlier while living in Des Moines. In 2014 Simon Conway, a talk show host for WHO Radio, broadcasted that he had recently taken a tour of the Reagans' simple 1800-square foot ranch home. He noted that the space was somewhat spartan, with only two pieces of art on the walls. Hanging in the Reagans' living room was a white-painted wooden board with the words "MOONLIGHT INN" printed in black letters.

ATKINS WEAVER HOUSE | 331 28TH STREET

Affectionately known as "The Seashell House" due to the eye-catching scallop shell motif carving over its front door, the home at 331 28th Street was built in 1900 and immediately attracted the attention of *House Beautiful* magazine in 1901. It was designed in the Medieval Rectilinear style with Gothic and Renaissance details by Liebbe, Nourse, and Rasmussen for James Bellamy Weaver and Fayette (Fay) Atkins Weaver.

James Bellamy Weaver was an attorney and the namesake of his father, a well-known politician, James Baird Weaver, who served non-consecutive terms in Congress from 1879 to 1881 and 1885 to 1889. The elder Weaver ran for United States

President in 1880 as part of the Greenback Party, securing 308,578 votes. He ran again in 1892 as a People's Populist Party candidate and received an impressive 1,041,021 votes, but ultimately lost to Grover Cleveland. His son also pursued a political career and in 1917 was voted into the Iowa House of Representatives, where he fought for quality education and the expansion of public schools. As a supporter of the arts, he also played a seminal role in securing funding for the founding of the Des Moines Art Center. He was honored for outstanding service to the community by the *Des Moines Register and Tribune*.

Fay Atkins Weaver was an artist who studied at the Cumming School of Art and received continued training in wood carving throughout the years. She designed and created many of the ornate details at 331 28th Street, including the dragons on the north and south gables, carvings on beams and around the fireplaces, and custom furniture created for the home - much of which is still in the original rooms for which it was designed. [See Artists of Owl's Head for additional information]. James and Fay's grandnephew, Hank Ketcham, was the creator of the famed comic strip "Dennis the Menace."

Above: A quote on the western-facing beam dividing the piano room and living rooms reads, "I had rather than forty schillings, I had my Books" and is adapted from Shakespeare's play The Merry Wives of Windsor, Act 1, Scene 1. The east side of the beam reads, "When a new book comes out, read an old one," adapted from the journals of Ralph Waldo Emerson, Volume XIII, 1852-1855.

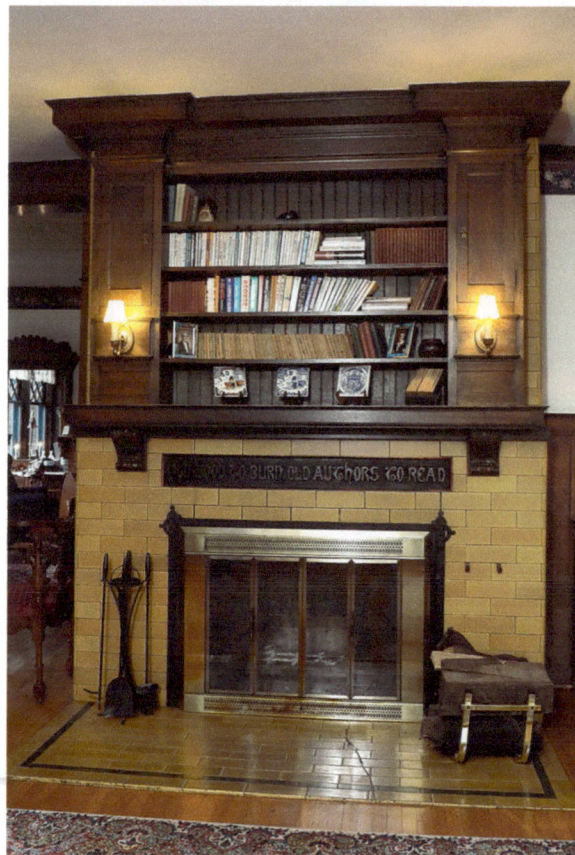

Far Left: In the master bedroom, Fay Weaver designed and executed the zodiac panels surrounding the fireplace and above the mantel using a method called pyrography (a technique of decorating wood by burning a design on the surface with a heated metallic point).

Left: Fay Weaver created the quote above the fireplace using pyrography. Originally written by Francis Bacon in the 1600s, it reads, "OLD WOOD TO BURN, OLD AUTHORS TO READ". Readers Digest Little Blue Books on the bottom shelf are from the early 1900s and are original to the home.

> " *I saved a real egg until it got pretty rotten. On Halloween night I planned to throw it at a neighbor's son as a prank. Just as I threw it, a car came along between us . . .*

Right: The leaded glass window that once held images of Persis and Eastman. Persis Weaver Robertson had the images removed and replaced with clear glass when she took ownership of the home.

ATKINS WEAVER HOUSE (CONT.)

This home was eventually passed down to the Weavers' daughter, Persis Weaver Robertson, who along with her husband, Albert, raised two daughters, Persis (Timmy) and Madeline (Maudy), there. When the elder Persis was growing up, she was always disturbed by the images of her and her brother, Eastman, featured in the stained-glass window going up the main stairway. She viewed herself as plain and her brother as much more appealing, so upon taking ownership of the home she immediately removed the images from the glass. Therefore, today the stained-glass window features two clear glass ovals where the Weaver children's images once resided. Persis Robertson inherited her mother's talent for art and from 1932 to 1933 attended the Stone City Art Colony, where she learned lithography. Her works were featured in group shows at the Art Institute of Chicago, the Library of Congress,

and the Brooklyn Museum. The Smithsonian American Art Museum owns one of her lithographs entitled Front Door. [See Artists of Owl's Head chapter for additional information]. Upon making contact with the home's current owners in the 1980s, Tom and Lorraine May, Persis sent a newly-created paper collage of fish entitled "Some Fishy Things" as a gift for the current owners' daughters, perhaps in tribute to the fond memories she had of growing up in Owl's Head.

Persis Robertson Gow (Timmy), remembered living in Owl's Head fondly. She had been one of four students at the private school taught by Hannah and Sarah Nollen at the corner of 29th and Grand Avenue. She recalled pranks the children played on Halloween:

"As Halloween approaches, I remember we had two nights . . . the 30th was "beggars night" (trick or treat) and the 31st was a night for mischief, of all sorts, which included soaping of windows, and woe to the household which left a full trash barrel outside . . . now, I expect, we would be hauled in for misdemeanors. Standard costumes were ghost-sheets and whatever else could be conjured up. I saved a real egg until it got pretty rotten. On Halloween night I planned to throw it at a neighbor's son as a prank. Just as I threw it, a car came along between us . . . window open . . . and the driver got the full brunt of the egg . . . in his face. Turned out he was a special delivery postal worker, who collared me, took me home to my waiting grandfather, and indicated that I should apologize and never dare to play another Halloween prank. I think I behaved after that."

ATKINS WEAVER HOUSE (CONT.)

The kids played hide and seek in the woods behind the homes on 29th Street. She also vividly remembered playing cards, a game called "Michigan" that went on for ages, on neighborhood porches, as well as the kindness that neighbors always showed to those in need. One story in particular left a lasting impression on her:

"The crossing of 28th Street by the railroad track was the last crossing before getting into town and therefore the best place for hobos to detrain . . . which they did . . . and came up the hill, seeking mostly food and sometimes warm and dry clothing. The telephone pole at the end of our driveway had markings on it which indicated that it was a good house to get help. Don't forget this was during the 1929 depression."

Descendants of the Weavers continued to own the home until it was sold in 1953 to Josephine and Horace Strong. The Strongs sold it to the Mays in 1984. Lorraine May is a highly respected attorney who trailblazed the path for female attorneys in Des Moines.

The Mays have made some updates to the home, such as remodeling the kitchen, renovating the carriage house with transformation of the third-floor hay loft into an office, and repurposing the third-floor ballroom into a roller rink and then a home theater. But they have maintained the home in tribute to its original artistic vision of the Weavers. Some custom furniture designed and customized by Fay Weaver remains in the dining room. The original fainting couch is still available in the front room for anyone needing to relax. Fay's artistic vision is still a strong theme in the home, with her engraving in the wood next to the fireplace still proudly stating "Old wood to burn, old authors to read." She carved the astrological signs that can still be found around the master bedroom fireplace and was the mastermind behind the dragon carvings, seashell doorway, and other ornate details on the outside of the home.

Like the many homes in Owl's Head, this home has played host to weddings. In this case, there have been three. The first was the union of Persis Weaver to Albert Robertson in 1918, followed by Persis (Timmy) Robertson's marriage to David Gow in 1947. Most recently, in 2006, the Mays' daughter, Kelsey, held her nuptials at her childhood home.

Left and Above: The table, chairs, china hutch and corner cabinet at the dining room are original to the home and were custom designed for the Weaver family.

Right: Aerial view of the property, 2019. There was a two-story addition to the back of the house, expanding the kitchen on the first floor and creating a new den on the second floor.

SUTHERLAND HOUSE | 2800 RIDGE ROAD

Constructed in 1905, the home at 2800 Ridge Road is one of the first visitors see as they approach the Owl's Head neighborhood from the north on 28th Street, standing on the aptly-named road along the edge of the neighborhood's highest point. It was first owned by Lial C. and Alice May Sutherland, who purchased the lot on July 30, 1903 for $3,500. The Sutherlands, along with Charles E. Mesmer, owned the Sutherland Milliner Company located in the Sutherland building on 10th Street. Lial was also president of the Sutherland Novelty Co. and Sutherland-Flenniken Co.

Built by C. C. Cross and Sons, the home features numerous elements of typical Georgian Revival design such as a gabled roof, window symmetry, center door placement, multi-paned windows, and clapboard siding. The grand entrance is embellished with a pediment, columns, and transom window above the door and has been featured on the cover of *Midwest Living magazine*.

The beautiful home interior includes meticulously maintained original oak woodwork in the living and dining rooms. However, in the dining room, a small cigarette burn mark can be found in the built-in buffet that is believed to have been left by famed musician Louis Armstrong when he was a guest in the home. As one of the most influential performers of jazz music and one of the great influencers of swing music, Armstrong and his band toured from 1920 to 1960. Bernie and Gloria Lowe, who were jazz lovers, hosted Armstrong on multiple occasions when they owned the home. Armstrong was well known to have performed at various events in Iowa in the 1940s. Some of his most famous Iowa performances were at the Surf Ballroom in Mason City, at the 1940 Iowa State Fair in Des Moines, and inside Des Moines' Salisbury House in 1949. [See A Musical Guest chapter for more on Louis Armstrong].

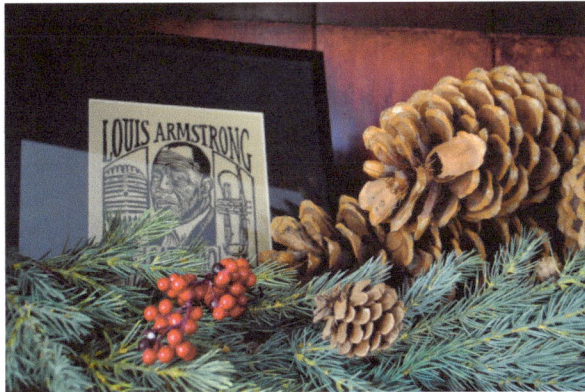
Right: The carriage house was designed with a unique curved roof, 2019

Below: Drawing honoring Louis Armstrong who was a frequent guest when the Lowe's owned the home, 2017

SUTHERLAND HOUSE (CONT.)

Above Left: Interior view of the front entry, 2019

Above Right: Living room with bay window, 2019

Below Left: Built-in buffet at the dining room, 2019

Below Right: The antique ceiling fan in the porch was believed to be the first ceiling fan installed in Des Moines, 2019

On the three-season porch there is an antique ceiling fan, rumored to have been delivered from New Orleans. Because ceiling fans were not common in the Midwest at this time, it is believed that this is the first ceiling fan to have been installed in Des Moines and was installed at the urging of visiting jazz musicians from New Orleans who frequented the home. It was not uncommon for these jazz musicians to stay in Owl's Head at this home when they performed in the Des Moines area.

The Arena Football League (AFL) was founded in this home when it was owned by Jim Foster from 1994 to 2002. Foster was a former National Football League (NFL) and United States Football League (USFL) executive and was later the principal owner of both the Iowa Barnstormers and the AF2's Quad City Steamwheelers. Many prominent figures in the football world spent time at this home during the time Foster lived in Owl's Head. Foster also served on the Iowa State Historical Society Foundation Board from 1998 to 2002 while living in Des Moines.

Left: Louis Armstrong and Bernie Lowe, Sr. at the neighborhood Herbie Pulis Grocery parking lot located at 35th Street and Rollins in Des Moines.
Photo courtesy of Bernie (Skip) Lowe III.

Far Right: Armstrong, Lowe, and Herbie Pulis clowning around at the neighborhood Herbie Pulis Grocery. The specific occasion for Armstrong's visit on this day is unknown - perhaps for a local club performance or playing at the Iowa State Fair, ca. 1940. Photo courtesy of Bernie (Skip) Lowe III.

Right: Louis Armstrong and Bernie Lowe, Sr. at the neighborhood Herbie Pulis Grocery parking lot located at 35th Street and Rollins in Des Moines. The car behind them was Lowe's 1937 Nash Convertible, ca. 1940. Photo courtesy of Bernie (Skip) Lowe III.

A MUSICAL GUEST

Bernie Lowe, Sr. was a professional drum player in the 1920s and was conductor of his own orchestra, Bernie Lowe & His Orchestra. The well-known band played in numerous ballrooms across the Midwest, including The Inn at Okoboji, Iowa Lake, The Val Air, The Surf, and many more.

In the early 1930s, Lowe fell in love with Gloria Means, whom he married in 1935. His father-in-law, George Means, felt his new son-in-law needed a real job, something steady to support a family. With that, Lowe got a job working with Des Moines Dry Ice Company, which he later purchased. He and Gloria were married for 32 years and had three children: Bernie Jr., Geoffrey, and Timothy.

Although Lowe was no longer playing professionally, he had developed quite a reputation as a talented musician, playing with the likes of Gene Krupa in the 1930s to 1940s. Lowe's skill set later inspired other great musicians such as Buddy Rich. His love of music kept him tight with local musicians and the music world. He met Louis Armstrong in 1928 while on tour in the Midwest, and they became fast friends. Lowe, always the life of the party and at ease talking with anyone, earned the nickname "Gator" from Armstrong. Armstrong had noted that Lowe was always talking and "had his mouth open like an alligator." The name Gator was eventually shortened to "Gate" and was a nickname Lowe used throughout the remainder of his life.

Armstrong played gigs in Iowa with regularity, and as a person of color in the 1940s was racially discriminated against by hotels. Lowe invited Armstrong to stay with his family in Owl's Head at 2800 Ridge Road on numerous occasions, and Armstrong became a familiar face in the neighborhood. Gloria Lowe always spoke fondly of Armstrong, remembering him as a gentle and sweet man. Lowe's and Armstrong's friendship lasted for decades until Lowe passed away in 1967. Shortly after Lowe's death, Armstrong was interviewed on National Public Radio. Before beginning the interview, Armstrong asked if he could make a tribute to his late friend and fellow musician, Bernie Lowe. He proceeded to play Taps live on air - a touching and heartfelt tribute to their friendship. [See the Sutherland House for more on the connection between Bernie Lowe and Louis Armstrong].

Left: Dite Myers holding Armstrong's trumpet despite never playing the trumpet himself. As a friendly joke, Armstrong wrote "To Dite- the world's greatest trumpet player." This photo appeared on the front cover of Down Beat Magazine. Myers said about Armstrong, "I loved the guy!" Copyright 2000 by William John Peverill.

Below Left: Armstrong played in various venues in Iowa in the 1940s, including the Surf Ballroom, State Fair, and Salisbury House.

Below: Des Moines Tribune article mentioning Lowe's death and Armstrong's National Public Radio tribute. Note that the article was written by Elizabeth Clarkson Zwart, who grew up in Owl's Head at 2750 Forest Drive and was also a friend of Louis Armstrong.

"

I looked up and felt so privileged that I had a chance to just watch him by myself. It was like being alone with [J.S.] Bach!

Lowe's love of music was passed down to his grandson, Bernie Lowe III (Skip, a.k.a. "Little Gate"), who is also a talented and professional percussionist. Like his grandfather, Skip realized at one point that he needed a full-time gig to support his family. Keeping things in the family and among neighbors in Owl's Head, Skip purchased his father's business, which had been previously purchased from another Owl's Head neighbor, Bill Prouty. Skip is currently the owner and CEO of Bernie Lowe and Associates, Inc. He will undoubtedly remain there until his next gig - perhaps joining a big band, and maybe in another life taking lessons from his grandfather!

Jack Peverill, who grew up in Des Moines, recalls having several interactions with Armstrong over the years. A particularly memorable evening took place around 1954, when Jack would have been about 21 years old. He and other family members went to the Val Air Ballroom in Des Moines to hear Armstrong play. Peverill's uncle Dite (Dwight) Myers, who grew up in Des Moines but at that time lived in Chicago, was a vocalist and friend of Armstrong's. Myers performed on stage with Armstrong and the band that evening. After the show, Peverill, Myers, Armstrong, and others went over to Bernie Lowe's home in Owl's Head at 2800 Ridge Road, where they "joked around, played records, and enjoyed dinner of fried chicken and beer." Myers and Armstrong always enjoyed reminiscing about times past. Myers served as an honorary pallbearer at Armstrong's funeral in 1971.

Peverill has fond memories of seeing Armstrong later on in life as well, such as the time he visited him in Springfield, Massachusetts. Both of them were sitting in the dressing room before a show and Armstrong said, "Let's go out and dig this roller-skating act." Peverill notes that Armstrong was like a little kid, and was as charming and jovial in private as he was on stage. They went out into the audience, and the band started playing the waltz "Over the Waves" while the skaters performed. Armstrong, who had his trumpet in his hand as they stood in the audience, lifted it to his lips and played along with the music, completely absorbed by the melody. Jack recalls: "I looked up and felt so privileged that I had a chance to just watch him by myself. It was like being alone with [J.S.] Bach!" [See An Unlikely Neighbor chapter for more on the Peverill Family connections to Owl's Head].

Several years later, in 1961, Peverill was in San Juan, Puerto Rico, where he knew Armstrong was going to be playing in one of the local hotels on New Year's Eve. Peverill and his wife went to the performance and afterward went up to Armstrong's room and rang in the new year with him, his wife Lucille, and three others.

Peverill's older brother, William Peverill, never met Armstrong but had a fascination with him and his influence on jazz music. W. Peverill wrote numerous stories about his family connections to Armstrong and about Armstrong's life. More on these stories can be found at https://www.Amherst.edu/.users/A/eadzima/wjpeverill52.

William and Jack's mother, Tine Myers Peverill, was also a friend of Armstrong's and was dancing the Charleston with him in Florida on the day Martin Luther King, Jr., was assassinated.

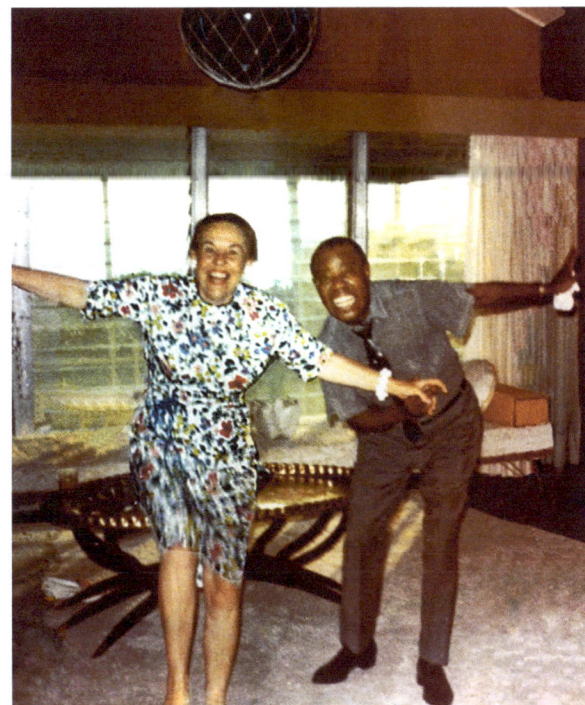

Above: Tine Myers Peverill with Louis Armstrong. Copyright 2000 by William John Peverill

Far Right: Home exterior, 2015

Right: Early advertisement of home at 2804 Ridge Road, Midwestern Magazine 1907

COURTESY OF LIEBBE, NOURSE & RASMUSSEN
Arthur Reynold's Residence on Ridge Road

REYNOLDS HOUSE | 2804 RIDGE ROAD

One of Owl's Head's largest homes, the 2 ½-story Gabled Cottage residence at 2804 Ridge Road was built in 1904 by successful Des Moines banker Arthur Reynolds and his wife, Bertha (Goodrich) Reynolds, shortly after they were married. Reynolds managed the Des Moines National Bank, increasing its deposits more than tenfold under his leadership, making it one of the largest in Iowa by 1915. He was offered a job as vice president at Continental and Commercial National Bank in Chicago and quickly rose to the role of bank president. He went on to lead the bank through two mergers and become the first bank president in the world to oversee resources in excess of $1 billion.

In 1911, prior to moving to Chicago, the couple designed an even-larger Des Moines home at 180 37th Street and sold the Ridge Road property to William R. Prouty. Previously in the dry goods business with W.K. Bird's dry goods store, Prouty had become a partner in his brother's wholesale business in 1873. The business was incorporated as C. C. Prouty Wholesale Grocery Co. in 1893. In 1911, after his brother died, Prouty became president of the company. The company prospered until it was destroyed by fire in 1930, gutting the four-story brick warehouse at 113 Third Street. Rather than rebuild, Prouty sold the business and retired. He passed away two years later in 1932 at age 74. His wife, Madge Prouty, continued to live in the house on Ridge Road until the early 1950s.

The large carriage house on the property was the original carriage house for the neighborhood and is presumed to have been built at the same time as the house, or shortly thereafter. It was designed with narrow clapboards and round arched windows above the doors, making it function superbly as the charming guest house it is today.

The home originally had a formal covered porch at the front entry that was connected to the large wrap-around porch on the side of the house. The front porch, much to the dismay of architecture enthusiasts and preservationists, was removed in later years. The spacious house is filled with light and, unlike many of the homes built in the early 1900s, has an open floor plan.

Above Far Left: *Front entry, 2015*

Above Left: *Living room, 2015*

Below Far Left: *Dining room with custom Sticks dining table, 2015*

Below Left: *Kitchen island featuring custom Sticks design, 2015*

Right: *Third-floor art studio for Sarah Grant, 2015*

REYNOLDS HOUSE (CONT.)

Bruce and Beverly Campbell bought the home in 1976. Bruce attended Harvard Law School and worked in Des Moines for 43 years at the law firm Thoma, Schoenthal, Davis, Hockenberg & Wine, today known as Davis Brown Law Firm. As was the case for a number of Owl's Head's past and present residents, Bruce taught courses at Drake University.

Fredrick S. Hubbell and his wife, Charlotte, moved their family from 2832 Ridge Road to 2804 Ridge Road in 1987. Hubbell was born and raised in Iowa and received his J.D. from the University of Iowa College of Law. In addition to working as an attorney, he has been a prominent businessman and politician. In 1983 he began working for Equitable of Iowa Companies, a life insurance company founded by his great-great-grandfather, Frederick M. Hubbell, in the 1860s. He became chairman of Equitable's Younkers Department Store in 1985 and in 1987 became Equitable's president.

In 2009, Hubbell was appointed acting director of Iowa's Department of Economic Development by Governor Chet Culver. Hubbell went on to become the Democratic Party nominee for governor of Iowa in 2018. In addition to his business activities, he has volunteered on numerous nonprofit boards and has donated to many philanthropic organizations. Charlotte is an independent writer and editor who has served on the Iowa Environmental Protection Commission. Together the couple formed the Fred and Charlotte Hubbell Foundation, which awards grants to numerous organizations both in Des Moines and nationally.

Sarah Grant purchased the home from the Hubbells in 1999. The open space on the third floor was the ideal location for the Ames native's art studio. Grant, who earned her BFA, MA and MFA from the University of Iowa studying under Mauricio Lasansky -- among other noted artists, is an accomplished fine art painter focused on Abstract Expressionism.

In 1987 Sarah was asked by a Meredith Corporation editor, Carol Dahlstrom, to design a wooden Nativity set that took her career in a new direction and inspired Sticks, Inc. Object Art and Furniture. As creator and owner of this now-nationally known brand, together with her fine art painting, Sarah Grant has achieved extraordinary success.

Grant made numerous creative updates to the home at 2804 Ridge Road, including a custom Sticks-style facade on the kitchen island, before selling the home in 2015. [See Artists of Owl's Head chapter for additional information on Sara Grant].

In 2019, Fred and Charlotte's daughter Meredith (Hubbell) Stahl and her husband, Andrew, purchased her childhood home and began raising their children in the house. One of the many wonderful testaments to growing up in Owl's Head is that former residents continue to return home to this genteel neighborhood.

Dr Walter L. Bierring.

RESIDENCE OF DR. WALTER L. BIERRING

HARBACH HOUSE | 2840 RIDGE ROAD

The construction of the elegant home at 2840 Ridge Road was set against the backdrop of exponential national growth in transportation technologies -- the development of the Ford Model A, the debut of the Indianapolis 500, and the ill-fated voyage of the Titanic. In Des Moines, Owl's Head was quickly becoming a desired location because of its proximity to the Ingersoll Avenue streetcar, which had a direct line back and forth from the city's major businesses and downtown attractions. The original owners of this home, Wilmot and Grace (Rawson) Harbach, purchased the land in 1910 for $3,500. They took out a total mortgage for $7,000, and it is believed that the final purchase price for the house was approximately $3,500.

Walking up the steps to this charming Dutch Colonial Revival, one immediately notices the distinctive porch design with ionic columns supporting a second-story balcony.

The urns located on the balcony corner posts represent a unique design feature not seen elsewhere in Owl's Head. The home design includes common characteristics of a Dutch Colonial Revival such as a gambrel roof, cedar shingle siding at the second story, overhanging eaves, a small porch, a balcony, and bay windows.

In 1913, The Harbachs sold the home to Dr. and Mrs. Walter L. Bierring. Walter Bierring earned his Doctor of Medicine from the University of Iowa in 1892. He was an influential physician in Iowa, leading the Iowa Public Health Association for 28 years. In addition to running his own private practice, he held numerous titles for his leadership in the national medical field during the course of his career. Among the contributions he made: he was a founding member of the Federation of the State Medical Boards; he helped organize the American Board of Internal Medicine and American Board of Preventive Medicine and Public Health; and he served both as president of the American Medical Association and Iowa's Commissioner of Health.

HOW THE WEBSTERS SPEND THEIR MONEY
Average monthly income, $741

(Based upon last year's gross income of $8900. Ben Webster's income depends upon volume of law business. This year he hopes to make about $10,000. Extra income will help pay off old obligations.)

Food	$160.00
Clothing	35.00
Mortgage, house taxes ($65 previous house, $137 now; monthly average last year)	101.00
Fuel, light and water	56.00
Maid and baby sitters	40.00
Insurance	45.00
Recreation and entertaining	40.00
Furniture and appliances	30.00
Club dues	4.00
Dancing lessons, books, magazines, records, flowers	18.00
Telephone	7.00
Medical and dental	20.00
Car expenses	25.00
Vacation fund	15.00
Cigarettes	12.00
Church and charities	15.00
Gifts	20.00
House repairs and upkeep (a minimum)	20.00
Dry cleaning, shoe repair, Ben's shirts	12.00
Income taxes	85.00
Total	**$760.00**

In 1955, Walter, now a widower, sold the home to Bennett and Elizabeth (Betty) Webster for $19,350. In 1956, the Ladies Home Journal was publishing a series on "How America Lives" and featured the Webster Family in its November issue. At that time Ben was a young attorney working for a law firm in Des Moines, while Betty was at home with three young daughters-- Susan, 7; Catherine, 5; and Elizabeth, 3-- with a fourth baby on the way. Purchasing the property at the price they paid (more than double Ben's $8,000 yearly salary) was a stretch for the young couple, but they had fallen in love with the 3-story, 6-bedroom home on Ridge Road. With a 40-foot ballroom on the third floor, there was ample room for their growing family to play.

Ben quickly emerged as a prominent lawyer and with his interest in politics was appointed state Republican Party chairman. Well-spoken and passionate about politics, Ben was chosen as a speaker for the Republican National Convention in 1964.

Betty was also actively involved in politics and chaired the campaigns for her Owl's Head neighbor, Julia Gentleman, when Gentleman successfully ran for Iowa House and Senate. She also served on the board for Planned Parenthood of the Heartland for many years.

In 1998, the property was sold to Mark and Eva Sherinian, where they raised their family. Mark had grown up in Owl's Head at the house on 2839 Forest Drive, which is located directly behind the property. With six bedrooms, a ballroom, and a sprawling yard, children have always been a big part of the story of this home. From Ladies Home Journal profiling the Websters and their young family, to the Sherinian Family raising a second generation of Owl's Head kids, to the current family being a part of the Owlettes (a neighborhood parent group that connects and shares advice), this enchanting home at 2840 Ridge Road was meant for family.

JAEGER MANUFACTURING CO.

Do High Grade Interior Woodwork
of all Kinds

Their work may be seen in a great many of the most exclusive and beautiful homes in the middle west, also the big office and store buildings. When you need work of this kind, why not have it done right. You run no risk in letting us do it for you.

Jaeger Manufacturing Co.,   215-225 E. 3rd St.
                                         Des Moines, Iowa

CORLEY HOUSE | 2845 RIDGE ROAD

Round the northwest corner of Ridge Road for an impressive view of one of Owl's Head's most stately homes: 2845 Ridge Road. It was designed by the architecture firm Liebbe, Nourse, and Rassmussen and built for Dexter Corley and his family in 1904. The ornate home with unprecedented detail was advertised in The Midwestern by Jaeger Manufacturing, a purveyor of high-grade interior woodwork, shortly after it was built; it was later featured in the book Art Work of Des Moines.

The home sits on a flat lot with plenty of grass, making it a popular spot to host the very competitive croquet tournament at the annual Owl's Head Labor Day party. In fact, the yard is so spacious it was once home to a 9-hole golf course.

Steep gables pronounce the roofline, while medieval bargeboards provide unique detailing not seen on other homes in Owl's Head. A sprawling wrap-around porch is punctuated by brick piers with stone shields at the top. The carriage house continues the theme of gable peaks, providing a cohesive complement to the home's signature style.

Far Right: Original wall sconce at 2845 Ridge Road, 2020

Right: Medieval bargeboards provide ornate detailing to the home's gables at 2845 Ridge Road

CORLEY HOUSE (CONT.)

> *Trick-or-treaters were in for quite a scare when they heard a witch's cackle coming from the roof!*

The inside of the home features a marble fireplace and extensive Jaeger Manufacturing woodwork. A main floor library is home to matching dragon sconces, a decorative detail that lends unique charm. The kitchen and butler pantry were updated in 2005 and were featured in Des Moines HomeStyle magazine in early 2006.

The original owner, Dexter Corley, was born in Illinois in 1858 and worked as a life insurance agent for New York Life Insurance Company in Des Moines. He and his wife, Jessie, had one son: John. John was not born in the home, but inherited it from his parents and would go on to live there for two decades. Dexter, Jessie, and John are buried at the Des Moines Masonic Cemetery. Since the Corleys, only three other families have resided in the home.

Although they are small in number, the owners of this home have been big in character. Second owner Jack McFadyen was renowned for playing his bagpipes to kick off the Labor Day festivities. Long-time residents often refer to his Scottish songs as one of their best memories from Labor Day parties gone by. Former Des Moines resident Grace Sherer, donning her ruby slippers and "Wicked Witch of the West" costume, once climbed out of a second-floor bedroom window to take her post during the Halloween season. Trick-or-treaters were in for quite a scare when they heard a witch's cackle coming from the roof!

Owl's Head Historic District
Labor Day 1989

LABOR DAY PARTY

The residents of Owl's Head have always been a group that enjoys social gatherings, whether they be parties in the third-floor ballrooms, dinners in the formal living rooms, or more casual affairs on the front porches. The square block design of the neighborhood lends itself to regular encounters with neighbors walking dogs or taking strolls to the local shops on Ingersoll.

In the mid-to-late 1970s, the neighborhood was pulled together to register as a National Historic District and also had a neighborhood association. Long-time resident Julian Archer was the first association president. Owl's Head was officially registered as a National Historic District in 1978, and that same year the first official Labor Day party took place. Many neighbors had been getting together for major holidays such as Independence Day and Labor Day in years prior. But the formal Labor Day party continued non-stop for 42 years until 2020, when the COVID-19 pandemic was spreading across the U.S. and around the globe.

In the beginning, the entire neighborhood worked together to plan the yearly festivities, but over time planning responsibilities transitioned to each major street (29th, Ridge, 28th, and Forest) rotating the ownership of planning each year.

According to Archer, the structure of the Labor Day party has remained relatively unchanged over the years. All current and former residents are welcome, and over the last few years guests have been included for an additional fee. On Friday evening the festivities kick off with a cocktail party for adults held inside a home on the hosting street. Early Saturday morning, the hosting street is barricaded from cars passing through, and sometimes there is a fun run around the block. Long-time resident Ben Webster affectionately named the "Killer Croquet" tournament that commences early on Saturday and is often accompanied by bloody marys and breakfast treats. The tournament regularly extends through most of the morning and rewards the winning team with the coveted owl trophy that can be proudly displayed at the winner's home until next year's party. The original trophy was lost some years ago; however, a replacement trophy has been adopted since the year of the unfortunate loss.

The daytime activities can vary each year from talent shows to bike decorating and games for kids such as bobbing for apples or hula hooping. Snow cone stations or ice cream trucks delight the children as they wait for the fire truck to arrive. The fire truck typically arrives in the mid-afternoon and is certainly one of the most memorable Labor Day traditions. The firefighters and sometimes police officers give tours of the fire truck and police car.

The fire truck leads a procession of children on bikes, scooters, and strollers around the neighborhood several times and hands out candy while sounding its horn. In years past the fire truck has escorted convertibles and classic cars to provide more of a traditional parade feel. Saturday concludes with a potluck for all families. The hosting street provides the main dish while neighbors from the other streets provide sides and desserts. In 1990, *Better Homes and Gardens* magazine requested photos and recipes from the Labor Day party for a brief article about the tradition.

Current and former residents regularly list the Labor Day party as one of their favorite aspects of living in the neighborhood. Former resident Nicole Lozier recalls: "My husband didn't like to miss the croquet tournament. It may not have been by coincidence that he went back [to Owl's Head] for business over Labor Day after we moved out of state so he wouldn't miss the competition!"

Families love the fun runs, big rides, games, picnics, and the local fire truck. Additional highlights have included: Jack McFadyen waking up the neighborhood with his bagpipes, the "Owlympics," custom Labor Day Party T-shirts, and the adoption of Owl's Head Estates. Although the Labor Day party was cancelled for the first time in 2020 due to pandemic concerns, residents are confident the party will continue for many years to come.

Opposite: Group photo at 2833 Forest Drive, 1989

Left: Scottish bagpipe group entertains at the Labor Day parade, 1990's

Below Left: Ted Stuart, Reece Stuart, and Joe Paulson play croquet at 2832 Ridge Road, 1970s

Below Middle: The first place winners of the annual Killer Croquet Tournament, Jennifer Kozlowski, John Stenberg, Davidson Kozlowski, and Peter Sherinian in front 2845 Ridge Road, 2018

Below Right: The Stender-Custer Family taking advantage of the ice cream truck parked in the neighborhood, 2019

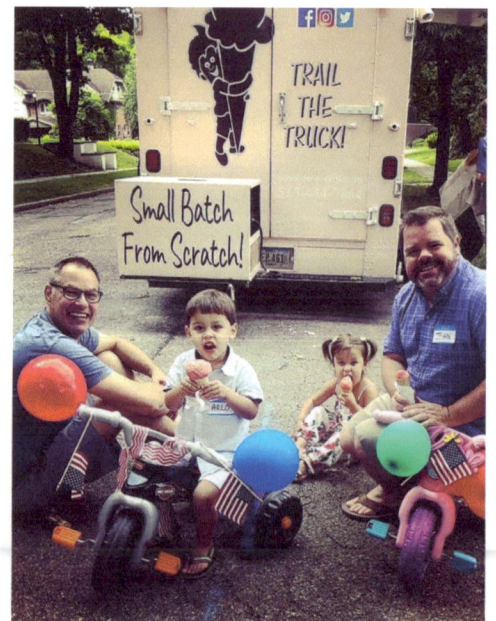

Right: Group photo taken at 338 29th St., 2006

Below Right: Floats for the annual parade, 1990s

Below Left: Arnold Garson driving the Spitfire, with daughter and friends in the convertible section of the parade, 1989

Below: Sophie Hamilton, Caroline Muelhaupt, and Dane Ashmore attend the Labor Day Party, 2019

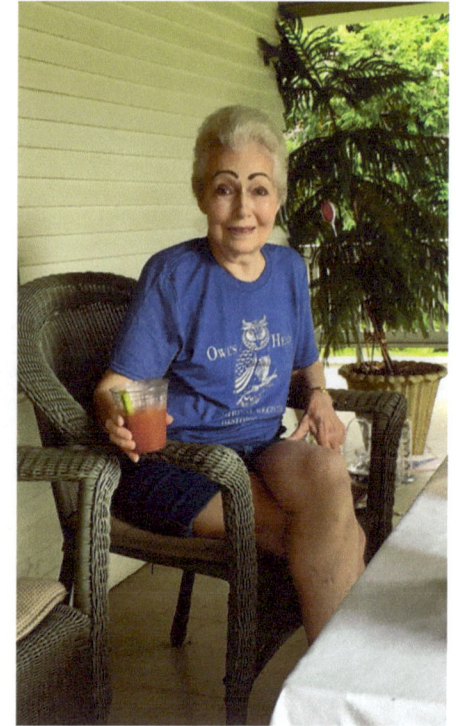

Above Left: The Owl's Head kids look forward to the annual visit by the local fire station

Above Right: Jane Archer enjoys a drink on the porch at 2845 Ridge Road, 2018

Below Left: Jackson Fisher, Guy Cook, and John Cook escort kids around the neighborhood during the parade

Below Right: Axel Sand joins the parade on his decorated bicycle, 2019

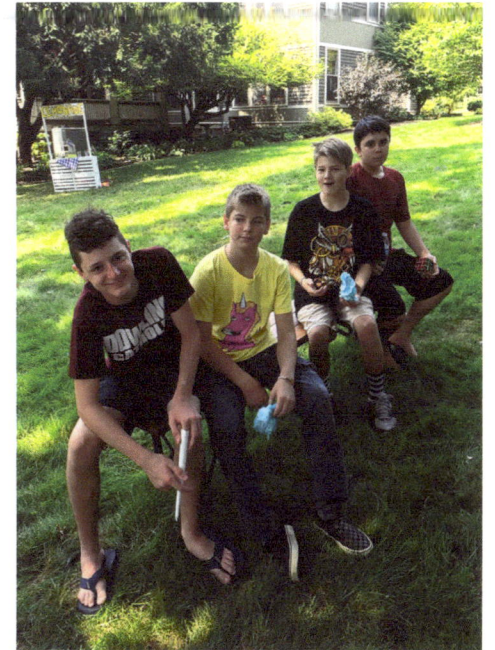

*Above Right: Celebrating in the backyard at 2832
Ridge Road, 1976*

*Above Left: Killer Croquet Tournament at 2839 Ridge
Road, 2019*

*Below Right: Nash Fisher, Chase Kozlowski, Drake
Ashmore, and Joseph Muelhaupt, a.k.a. The Owl Squad,
at the 2017 Labor Day Party on Forest Drive*

*Below Left: Meredith (Hubbell) Stahl and daughter
Evelyn enjoying the Labor Day Party, 2019*

Houses in Owl's Head

ADDRESS	YEAR BUILT	ORIGINAL OWNERS	ARCHITECTURAL STYLE
2800 Ridge Road	1905	Lial and Alice Sutherland	Georgian Revival
2804 Ridge Road	1904	Arthur and Berta Reynolds	Gabled Cottage
2808 Ridge Road	1966	Glenn and DeLoise Witt	Ranch
2815 Ridge Road	1907	G. C. Hubbell	Medieval Rectilinear
2825 Ridge Road	1905	E. J. Davidson	Maheresque
2830 Ridge Road	1898	C. Witmer	Gabled Cottage
2831 Ridge Road	ca. 1905	C. H. Philpott	Gabled Cottage
2832 Ridge Road	ca. 1895	M. E. Kinne	Simplified Queen Anne
2839 Ridge Road	1907	H. F. Graefe	Medieval Rectilinear
2840 Ridge Road	ca. 1910	Wilmer and Grace Harbach	Dutch Colonial Revival
2845 Ridge Road	ca. 1904	D. W. Corley	Medieval Rectilinear
2848 Ridge Road	ca. 1900	Sedgwick S. Brinsmaid	Maheresque
304 29th Street	1904	John A. Baal	Undefined
320 29th Street	1904	W. A. Guild	Maheresque
330 29th Street	1907	William H. and Frances Langan	Tudor
338 29th Street	1907	Thomas M. and Julia Langan	Medieval Rectilinear
402 29th Street	ca. 1916	Gerard and Mary Witmer	Georgian Colonial
446 29th Street	1895	*Bradshaw Family	Undefined
450 29th Street	ca. 1890's	W. W. Witmer	Farmhouse
451 29th Street	1910	George and Sarah Rowell	Undefined
2750 Forest Drive	1913-1914	J. S. Zwart	Medieval Rectilinear
2800 Forest Drive	1905	Caroline Lichty	Georgian Revival
2805 Forest Drive	ca. 1901	Craig T. Wright	Gabled Cottage
2814 Forest Drive	1905	Charles, Caroline, and Belle Gilcrest	Medieval Rectilinear

ADDRESS	YEAR BUILT	ORIGINAL OWNERS	ARCHITECTURAL STYLE
2829 Forest Drive	1890	William and Johanna Brecht	Rectilinear Queen Anne
2831 Forest Drive	1909	H. Clark	Medieval Rectilinear
2833 Forest Drive	1904	Henry Hewitt	Medieval Rectilinear
2834 Forest Drive	1898 or 1903	Thomas and Jeannette Stevenson	Undefined
2838 Forest Drive	1905	Oliver J. Fay	Gabled Cottage
2839 Forest Drive	1911	E. Hewitt	Medieval Rectilinear
2846 Forest Drive	1893	Nathan Emery Coffin	Richardsonian/Colonial Revival
2849 Forest Drive	1913	I . E. and Betsy Tone	Undefined
2900 Forest Drive	ca. 1900	W. J. Riddell	Undefined
2908 Forest Drive	1906	Harry Dustan Rawson	Gabled Cottage
302 28th Street	1955	Angus and Janice Campbell	Ranch
305 28th Street	1913	H. C. Downing	Gabled Cottage
313 28th Street	ca. 1885	James and Mary Watt	Undefined
331 28th Street	1900	James Bellamy Weaver/Fayette Atkins Weaver	Medieval Rectilinear
400 28th Street	1900	*A. L. Irwin	Medieval Rectilinear
401 28th Street	ca. 1892	*Ernest E. Clark	Shingle Style
407 28th Street	1902	George Cummins	Gabled Cottage
415 28th Street	1892	J.S. Gilcrest	Rectilinear Queen Anne
420 28th Street	1941	Warner Family	Undefined
425 28th Street	2007	Leslie and Vicki Beer	Undefined
428 28th Street	1914	Jacob E. Binkley	Undefined
431 28th Street	1914	G.D. Ellyson	Prairie School Influence
434 28th Street	1917	Alfred Bretchtel	Undecided
2900 Grand Avenue	1905	W. W. And Mary Witmer	Neo-Georgian Colonial

Believed to be the original owner, records are incomplete. Anyone with additional information is asked to please contact the authors at sondraashmoreink@gmail.com.

REFERENCES

Adams, Gordon. "The Governor's Home." The Iowan, Feb/Mar 1953.

Banger, Linda. "Meet Me on the Corner of 29th and Grand Avenue." Des Moines Register, March 19, 1997, p. 15AT-WSS.w

Brigham, Johnson. History of Des Moines and Polk County Iowa. The S.J. Clarke Publishing Company, 1911, v.1.

Bryson, Mary. A Modern Victorian. Des Moines Register, August 25, 1985, p. 1E.

Byrd, Lisa Lavia. "Revival Style." Metro Home and Real Estate, December 1997, p. 1.

Carlson, Kent. "Colonial Revival: Des Moines' Witmer House Comes Full Circle." Cityview, November 2016, pp 78-82.

Carroll, B. F. "Lafayette Young." The Annals of Iowa v. 15, 1927, pp. 590-597.

Cochrane, Diane. "Cornelis Ruhtenberg: Oriental Essence." American Artist Magazine, February 1974, pp. 26-29, 69.

Dahl, Orin L. Gilcrest Lumber Company: Everything in Lumber Provided by Des Moines' Oldest Firm. in Des Moines: Capital City, Centennial Heritage Inc., 1978.

"Delay Buying Home for Governor." Des Moines Tribune, September 20, 1947, p. 3.

Des Moines Planning and Zoning Commission. Des Moines Heritage: A Survey of Significant Architecture Phase II, Summer 1977.

DMPL Team, "Ronald Reagan in Des Moines," Project Des Moines, accessed December 15, 2020, https://projectdesmoines.dmpl.org/items/show/35.

Gale Research. American Decades Primary SourcesL 1980-1989 v. 9. Gale Publishing, 1998.

Gandelman, Claude. "Visible Language XXIII 2/3", Visible Language, Rhode Island School of Design, 1989, p. 299.

Gentleman, Gregor. A Brief History of 2814 Forest Drive, Owl's Head, and its Owners, date unknown.

Hoffman, Betty H. "How America Lives." Ladies Home Journal, November 1956, pp. 191-200.

Ingham, Vicki. Younkers: The Friendly Store, The History Press, 2016, pp. 11-27.

"Inghams in Washington." The Register and Tribune, February 17, 1909, p. 1.

"James Bellamy Weaver" The Annals of Iowa v. 22, 1940, p. 416.

"Lafayette Young." The Annals of Iowa v. 15, 1927, 630-632.

Lutz, Renda. "Divorce, Murder Charge Hit Homeowner." Des Moines Register, Feb. 2004, p. 4.

Lutz, Renda. "Meet Me On The Corner." Des Moines Register, February 20, 2002, p. 2W3.

Lutz, Renda. "Women Rallied to Cheer Up Soldiers." Des Moines Register, Feb. 2004, p. 6.

McGarvey, Carol. "It's the Season." Welcome Home Des Moines, November/December 2012.

McLaughlin, Lillian. "Widow of 'Mr. Drake' at Relays. . . Where Else?" Des Moines Tribune, April 1970, p. 18.

McMahan, Virgil. The Artists of Washington D.C., 1796-1996. Artists of Washington, 1995.

Mills, George. Harvey Ingham & Gardner Cowles, Sr. - Things Don't Just Happen. Iowa State University Press, 1977.

National Parks Service. "Owl's Head Historic District." National Register of Historic Places. https://npgallery.nps.gov/NRHP/AssetDetail/dfa974a0-2911-4000-a95e-cdc8d3542c94. Accessed November 2015.

Norvall, Kim. "Three Grand Avenue Apartments, once home to Ronald Reagan, Will Undergo a Historic Renovation." The Des Moines Register, June 16, 2020, https://www.desmoinesregister.com/story/money/business/development/2020/06/16/des-moines-development-grand-avenue-apartments-renovated/3197417001/ .

"Owl's Head." Des Moines Daily News, November 13, 1896.

"Persis Robertson." Smithsonian American Art Museum. https://americanart.si.edu/artist/persis-robertson-4078. Accessed December 2017.

"Persis Robertson." Wikipedia https://en.wikipedia.org/wiki/Persis_Robertson_Accessed May 2020

Persis Weaver Roberstson: When Tillage Begins: The Stone City Art Colony and School. projects.mtmercy.edu. Accessed December 2017.

Peverill, William.Stories from Pipa Bill. Amherst College. https://www.amherst.edu/users/A/eadzima/wjpeverill52. Accessed October 19, 2020.

Selley, Zachariah. The Ralston Family Collection 1850-2000. Lewis & Clark College Special Collections and Archives, 2013. http://archiveswest.orbiscascade.org/ark:/80444/xv22479 Accessed March 2017.

Strong, Natalie. "The J.B. Weaver House." Term Report, May 1958.

The Midwestern v. 1-5 https://archive.org/details/The Midwestern Volume 1. Accessed July 2017.

Tone, Mary. Tone Bros., speech given at Captain Greeley Questers, November 1980.

Vande Haar, Dale A. "Ingham, Harvey." The Biographical Dictionary of Iowa.

Webster, Bennett. "Save Governor's Home by Rezoning." Des Moines Tribune, September 1975, p. 4.

Worthen, Thomas. Jules Kirschenbaum: The Need to Dream of Some Transcendent Meaning. University of Iowa Museum of Art, September 2006, pp 1-8, 55-56, 73-74.

ACKNOWLEDGEMENTS

This book would not have been possible without the generous and insightful contributions from the following people who supported our vision. Our gratitude extends far beyond what words can express.

CURRENT RESIDENTS: John Beard and Mark Harrington, Julian and Jane Archer, Kellie Hockmuth, Libby Muelhaupt, Burch and Rachelle LaPrade, Carey and Judi Ford, Tom and Lorraine May, Jean and Blair Hamilton, Ann Beneke, Tom and John Stender-Custer, Meredith Stahl, Ross and Alexandra Haeberle

FORMER RESIDENTS: Persis Gow, Fred and Anne Crane, Rob and Christine Sand, Lorn Matthews, The Webster Family, The Eddy Family, The Riley Family, Mindy Miller, Julie Gammack, Arnold Garson, Michelle LaBrecque, Rosalie Gallagher, Sarah Grant, Kate Bruns, Fred and Charlotte Hubbell, Peter Sherinian, Nicole Lozier, Julia Gentleman, The Carpenter Family

OTHER CONTRIBUTORS: John Tone, Bill Ralston, Purr Whalley, Jack Peverill, Bernie (Skip) Lowe III, Sarah Swenson

Left: Dr. Julian and Jane Archer led the efforts for Owl's Head neighborhood to become recognized as a National Historic District in 1978. Historic designation signs were installed on utility posts by Julian and neighborhood kids in 2019.

AUTHORS AND ILLUSTRATOR

Sondra Ashmore, husband Brian, and sons Drake and Dane have enjoyed being Owl's Head residents at 338 29th Street since 2014. She received her bachelor's degree in communications at Iowa State University, master's degrees at Rensselaer Polytechnic Institute in technical communication and management, and her Ph.D. at Iowa State in Human Computer Interaction. She publishes on software development best practices and methodologies and co-authored the book Introduction to Agile Methods. She has spent her career in the field of technology and is passionate about old homes and historic preservation. She was a member of the Des Moines Historic Preservation Committee.

Christine Guzzo Vickery worked as a healthcare interior designer in Minneapolis for 31 years before retiring in 2017. She grew up in southeastern Iowa and received her bachelor's degree from the University of Iowa. Her knowledge and interest in interior design and architecture were the reasons she became involved in writing about Owl's Head. In addition to co-authoring this book, she is also the author of the children's book: Nighttime in Owl's Head. She has co-authored two books on healthcare interior design: Modern Clinic Design: Strategies for an Era of Change and Clinic Design: Enhancing the Patient Experience through Informed Design. She has also published numerous family books, including a family history of her Sicilian ancestry: La Famiglia Domenico Guzzo: Eventi La Storia. She lives in Minnetrista, Minnesota with her husband, Peter, and daughter Mei. She is a proud aunt of Sondra Ashmore and enjoyed having the opportunity to work with her on this book.

Sharon Larson is a watercolor artist specializing in custom portraits of homes, farms, and pets. Her work has been recognized for its elaborate attention to detail with whimsical flair. She is also acknowledged as a gifted watercolor teacher, having taught at Blackhawk College and other venues. She received her bachelor's degree from the University of Wisconsin, Green Bay, where she studied English and writing. Since 1995 Sharon, her husband, and their three children have called Iowa their home. They now grow crops and care for a menagerie of animals on their Long Grove acreage. She's a member of the Beaux Arts executive committee, which helps support the Figge Art Museum in Davenport, Iowa. She's the illustrator of a children's book titled Cock-a-Doodle Don't, But Cock-a-Doodle Do and is the author of the eBook Growing Beautiful. To see her recent work or to request a painting, visit slarsonwatercolors.com or follow S. Larson Watercolors on Facebook.

*Susan Webster and Lorn Matthews with their homemade go-kart
outside of 2840 Ridge Road, ca. 1961*